THE CHILD DEVELOPMENT AND POSITIVE PARENTING MASTER CLASS

PROVEN METHODS FOR RAISING WELL-BEHAVED AND INTELLIGENT CHILDREN, WITH ACCELERATED LEARNING METHODS

BUKKY EKINE-OGUNLANA

TCECPUBLISHING.COM

Published by

TCEC Publishing

England, Great Britain.

CONTENTS

101 TIPS FOR CHILD DEVELOPMENT

101 TIPS FOR HELPING WITH YOUR CHILD'S LEARNING

101 TIPS FOR CHILD DEVELOPMENT

PROVEN METHODS FOR RAISING CHILDREN AND IMPROVING KIDS BEHAVIOUR WITH WHOLE BRAIN TRAINING

DEDICATION

This book is dedicated to our three amazing children and all the beautiful children all over the world who over the years have passed through the T. C. E. C 6-16 years programme. Thank you for the opportunity to serve you and invest in your colourful and bright future.

EDITOR'S PREFACE

I wouldn't believe you if you say you don't know about children. You either have some, or have had kids at some point, though they might be all grown now and left home. Even if you have no such experience, what about your childhood? At least we all get to start life as children.

Can't remember?

Okay, Bukky will help you play catch-up.

It's all here in this book.

All kids are born the same no matter how different our races, nationalities, tribes, or family socioeconomic standing. But how we all manage to turn out so differently in our social behaviours had long baffled scientists and psychologists around the world.

No more!

Today, behavioural scientists are churning out tons of explanations why Tom is Tom, Dick is Dick, and Harry is uniquely different, and why each child needs a unique approach when it comes to their development. Some of the explanations are plausible, while some are very odd.

What Bukky Ekine-Ogunlana has produced in this work is not a grand theoretical argument simply so she could join the array of theorists on children behaviours; instead, as wife, mother, educator and coach to children and teenagers, her several decades-long experiences has identified key issues affecting the proper social development of children and teens, both at home and at school. She treats the problems with a knowing tact that every parent and teacher can identify with.

Start early, she urges parents; and that leaves me with some gloom. Where have you been, Sister? If I knew this before I got married, I am sure I would have been better prepared to be the father you describe; and my wife sure would have done better too! Yes, some ground has been lost, and I presume this will be true for many folks; but there's still some room to adjust and do some repairs, aren't there, Bukky?

The assurances the author provides, and the route to navigate to reclaim lost ground – all practically illustrated – make the tips in this book a must-read for all prospective partners before they marry. Make the ideas in here the parenting bible for all expectant parents, for all new parents, then for the sweet or bruised parent of strong-willed children and rambunctious teenagers.

With the challenge of parenting so enormous in today's realities, *101 Tips for Child Development* is a help book, one that provides skills set that contributes to the training process of making children and teens independent, confident, successful and happy.

Readers of this book are sure to reflect on what had been, the mistakes made, and the broader effects of proper and improper actions taken regarding children. A drop of tears won't be out of place; but the author also expects many drops of the tears of joy, just for the fresh discovery and the opportunity to adjust and start doing right.

I'm involved!

O John

Managing Editor

(ICBN), L A

INTRODUCTION

Some children and teens are socially versed from birth; others struggle to adjust and live with various challenges that come with social acceptance. While some children and teens find it relatively easy to make good friends, others are loners. While some are inbuilt with self-control, others are hot-tempered. Some are born to be natural leaders. Others learn the skills to be true leaders, while others are withdrawn completely. Each child is born with a unique set of attributes that force parental figures to adapt to their specific needs.

In the past ten years, psychologists have been convinced that the essential skills needed for child development can be taught and should be learnt by parents. Previous studies have shown that children who were at a time shy can change and become outgoing, children who were once aggressive can master the art of self-control, just as children who isolate themselves can learn how to make friends with proper attention to specific areas of child development. There's no doubt that children and teens who were raised to be better persons have a significant advantage in life. Not only will they enjoy the rewards of positive relationships, these children usually have a better self-image and leave school having performed better than their peers.

Generally, these children are more resilient regardless of the challenges that life throws their way.

This book is designed for parents, carers and teachers to teach children and teens the crucial skills necessary for self-development. The book has 11 chapters, each addressing different skills required for development. There are 101 ways to develop your children and teens, with other 59 bonus tips to raise your children into happy and successful adults. Children and teens are expected to possess these skills to become better persons, useful at home, at school, and the community at large. The lessons put forward in this guide are intended to assist in instilling a greater sense of resilience and perseverance in children to encourage self-development. Children should be able to confront challenges and overcome them. Many children have lost direction because they have not been taught to endure, to withstand crisis, build stamina to endure and persevere or go through any adverse life situation.

As parents, we should aim to teach children to use their mind, to make them do things consciously and apply the brain in any critical situation, which is discretion: to think strategically. Parenting must be deliberate, purposeful, intentional with guiding principles.

You will often hear parents shouting to their children "Don't go over there" or "Don't touch that". It may work at the moment but unfortunately it's not encouraging the self-development discussed above. Relating this to the digital age of today, your child may be using a digital device like a tablet, it's essential that you avoid using the word 'don't'. Observe and give room for development as they learn how to apply their skills to correctly use the technology, they're going to get things wrong and click on the wrong things. Give them space and freedom to get things wrong and quietly observe as they find the solution.

Guiding, rather than commanding will assist in wholesome development. Commanding will only work at the moment and it's essential to think of the bigger picture. Children have an in-built ability to learn skills to become better, more well-developed versions of themselves, so give them the time to learn the skills themselves. Guiding where necessary without being overbearing. That is the crucial factor in enabling wholesome, positive development, allowing your child to thrive.

After reading this guide, please feel free to leave a review based on your findings and how useful the guide was to you. I would be incredibly thankful if you could take 60 seconds to write a brief review on the platform of purchase, even if it's just a few sentences!

DEVELOPING SOCIAL SKILLS

Social skills have proved essential for the development of children. Children who are less social can be bossy, impatient, or demanding. Such children may face a host of different issues later in life and become shy, not talk at all or talk too much. Children with improved social skills have certain abilities:

- They can break the ice; they can introduce themselves to anyone or invite someone to carry out an activity with them.
- They know how to manage conflict. Such children know how to compromise and stand up for themselves when unreasonable demand is requested of them.
- They show interest in their friends and other valuable relationships.
- Socially successful children make eye contact; they listen, and offer help.

In society today, children and teens are faced with obstacles and challenges that the earlier generations weren't opportune to experience. Looking at Today's world, technology and social media have taken the reins; as such, there is a need to observe the ways technology and social media have tampered with social interactions. In my experience as a teacher, I've heard students make statements like:

"I find it weird to talk to people over the phone; why should I do that?"

"I don't know what people think about me when I talk to them over the phone. "

I have since been putting different thoughts into the questions and issues raised by students, and have wondered: How can we, as teachers, carers, educators, parents and clinicians teach the younger generation the necessary social skills to have in a world where face to face interactions and communications are now so reduced?

Over time, I have compiled a list of ways by which teachers, carers and parents can teach and encourage healthy and appropriate social skills in children and teens to combat the adverse effects social media may be having on their developing mind.

DEVELOPMENT TIPS FOR CHILDREN:

1. Role Play Self-Introduction

A child would ask:

"How do I talk to someone that I know little or nothing about?"

"What do I say?"

"Do we have common interests?"

In role-play, self-introduction with your child, assume the role of your child and let the child take the role of the supposed "new friend" he/she is meeting. The role-play of self-introduction will further lead to several discussions and should hopefully lead to questions like,

"How do I invite a friend over to the house for a playdate or sleepover?"

"How do I join a game that's started already?"

2. Start a Game of Emotional Charades

More than often, face to face interactions for children with their peers are limited. As such, children are often finding it more difficult to read the emotional cues of others. For the game of emotional charades, write down different emotions on pieces of paper and give each emotion to each child. After this, you want to express or demonstrate the emotions across your face.

You can up the challenge by using other body parts to express the feelings. For instance, you can demonstrate or express the anger emotion by clenching your fists or cross your arms tightly on your chest. This will open an avenue for discussions and answer questions like:

"What are the situations that call for these emotions?"

"What do these emotions communicate?"

"How do you react to each emotional situation?"

Teach how to express emotions, let the child know the consequences of his or her actions which make others feel bad. Actions are connected to other people's feeling and create a world around them.

3. Match the Tone of Your Voice to an Emotion

This can be achieved in diverse ways, such as role-play, charades, voice recording and using examples from movies or TV shows. Sit with your child and identify all the emotions that are expressed and can be identified through the tone of voice of a person.

For instance, for sad emotion, a sad person will talk in a low or quiet tone. This will teach your child both how to register and read social cues others are giving off about their emotions, and how to react when they face those emotions in real life.

4. Practice Taking Turns

Being patient and taking turns is not a simple task for children. Consider filing a colouring sheet or playing a game by taking turns.

5. Use the Child's Interests

If you find that a child has an interest or hobby, use it as an advantage by discussing social skills that are related to that interest. For instance, if a child plays hockey, you can ask questions like,

"How do you think your hockey team can work together?"

"What can you do to improve the mood of someone who's having a bad game?"

You can also use a child's interest to organise playdates and help the child form relationships with other children outside of those interests.

Always pay attention and nurture the interest of your child. If your child has an interest in something, explore it; find out more about it so that the interest does not die. Take the example of hockey: the communities dedicated to it should be your point of focus. Devote more of your time to nurture this interest, and water it so the seed does not die. Interest is like a seed that should bring fruits out if they are planted and are well cultivated, else they will die.

FOR TEENS:

6. Volunteer for a Charity Work with Your Teen

Taking up a charity work with your teen will create an opportunity to work closely together. You can be precise and well assured that your teenager will follow your lead and example and in turn use the same etiquettes you used when working with his/her peers and other people.

7. Play a Game that Allows You to Say Anything

This game is a board game that allows you to answer questions whichever way you choose. This board game is a fun way of enhancing communication. As the teacher or parent, you can point out the emotions you observe in your teens when they were sharing the answers to the game. Answering question is one-way children discover the world around them.

8. Role Play Job Interview Skills

As a teacher, I have seen several teens who are anxious about the topic of a job interview. To ease this tension and anxiety in teens, provide a list of interview questions for role play. You play the role of the person being interviewed and your teen plays the role of the interviewer. From your answers to the interview questions, your teen will be able to create a visual example of how to engage interview questions correctly.

9. Write a Letter Seeking for Help

Instead of giving in to every request of your teen on the spot, ask him/her to write a letter to you seeking help. More often than not, writing out our needs and feelings affords us the chance to take a step back from what is causing the distress and focus on addressing how we feel and the things we need. Not only will this be helping your teen to practice the skill of seeking help, it will most certainly also help them to identify their needs. Both perform an essential role in your teen's success later in life.

10. Play the Awkward Moment Card Game

The awkward moment card game is an entertaining and fun game designed for teens. It engages scenarios that aren't comfortable, where the players have to submit a reaction to the uncomfortable scenarios. This game provides the opportunity for teens to talk about social situations that are not comfortable, and practice thinking on the spot on how to escape or deescalate the awkwardness of the situation.

YOUR FREE GIFT!

As a way of saying thank
your for
purchasing this book, I am
offer offering you a free
parenting book!

You can click on the link
below or you can wait until
the end of the book to collect
and download your free
copy.

**DOWNLOAD
YOUR FREE COPY
HERE**

SOCIAL SKILLS ACTIVITIES

Are you a concerned parent who wants to help your children develop excellent social skills? Then read this. It's imperative for children to have excellent social skills, as they help to prepare them for life ahead. The need to socialise and the way to socialise will change as soon as your child grows to become a teenager.

The teenage years are filled with rage, grumpiness and confusion stemming from puberty. Children with poor social skills may end up becoming emotionally distant teens. Most times, poor social skills will manifest as depression or rage. Kids who lack social skills will find it difficult to keep and maintain meaningful relationships when they grow into teenagers and adults. So, there is a need for parents to help their teens learn the appropriate social skills during this time to provide them with the building blocks they can use in the following years.

The bulk of the work is on the parents who will do a lot of good if they allow their children to participate in social activities. Below are some suggested games and activities to help your young kids and teens develop social skills as they transition through this stage in their life.

ACTIVITIES FOR TEENS

11. Theatre

A theatre is a great place for teens to meet diverse people and widen their horizons. Take a trip to the local theatre groups in your vicinity and inquire if they have open spots for teens, or encourage your teen to join their school's theatre group. The theatre is suitable for both children who are less social and provides plenty of benefits for those who are considered social already. The theatre may help your shy teen to open up and be confident. It can also help your social kid relate with different kinds of people in a creative environment. Teens who do not fancy being in the limelight can take a job in the production or costume unit of theatre companies.

Secondly, encourage your teen to participate in school plays. If you noticed, for example, that your child is a timid person but has real play skills, do you know what that kid needs?

Yeah!

Encouragement.

Taking him to the theatre often will go a long way in providing the needed support for the child. You could introduce the child to a playgroup that would help him/her. You really can't imagine how much the child would improve socially.

12. Activity Camps

Summer camps with lots of fun/engaging activities are ideal for children of all age groups. Search for a field that is ideal for your teen. Summer camp is an excellent place to meet and work with new people, make friends, and relate with strangers. Weekend or day camp is useful for teenagers who lack social skills. Just a day of connecting with new people and participating in different activities will help even the shy kid to learn valuable social interaction skills. There are various options for summer camps, including music, science, sports, dance, and drama.

13. Volunteer Work

Taking up volunteer work is an excellent activity for children of all age groups. Encourage your teenager to take up volunteer jobs at the animal shelter, child welfare centres and retirement homes. Also, you can encourage your teen to teach smaller kids useful skills or even read them books.

Help your teen understand that he/she can organise volunteer work to help the community or neighbourhood. While helping others, your teen is also improving his/her social skills. Volunteer work allows your child to see tangible results in their community and enhance their sense of self-worth.

14. Participating in Sports

There are reasons fitness experts advise that sports are essential. Teens can learn the value of fitness, teamwork, organisation, motivation, leadership and support while playing games. All these qualities combine to build the teen's character and improve social skills.

Sports also allow your children to understand the importance of dedication to a specific craft, a skill which transitions well into the workforce for years to come.

15. Art Classes

Besides nurturing the artistic talent of your teen, taking art classes also helps to improve their social skills. Not only will they get an outlet to express themselves, they will also find the opportunity to interact with fellow students and their instructors. Art classes can offer a fantastic chance for shy kids to air their views better through creativity. Motivate your teens to take up art classes and crafts in which they have some flair: fabric art, painting, pottery, sketching, and sculpture. These and similar activities help teens to express themselves beneficially.

16. Bonfire Night

Do not be a boring parent. Organise bonfire nights and plan events with your extended family members in attendance. Embolden your teenager to invite their friends to bonfire nights to have fun times with friends.

17. Educational Trips

So, you discovered that your teen loves visiting the museum. Great! Plan trips and activities that will allow him/her to improve on their social skills. Plan a trip for your teen to visit the museums in neighbouring towns. You can also help to further their interest by encouraging visits to bookstores where they can read historical books.

Make inquiries about seminars and lectures related to your teen's field of interest and sponsor the conference for your teen to go with a friend. Besides helping teens explore their interests, educational trips also provide teens with the opportunity to relate with new people. Asking a genuine question during the Question and Answer period of a lecture takes a great deal of gut from a teen.

18. Game Nights

A game night during a family event is a great and entertaining way to help teens open up to others. Make the activity even more exciting by asking visitors to come up with games on the spot. Then take a vote to select the best games. This bonding with others will help your teen to develop and improve social skills.

Game nights will also teach your children how to win and lose with class and dignity.

19. Live Events

No doubt, watching live events with friends or family members is a great experience for teens. The live event could be a dance performance, championship game, competition, quiz show, music recital or any other function of the sort. At live events, your teen would be within a crowd who are mostly strangers. Live demonstrations will help to douse the shyness in your teen who will have no choice but shout and cheer his/her favourite team.

20. Bowling Fun

Plan a night of ice skating, roller skating or bowling with your teen. The importance of this cannot be overstressed. Such visits will help to improve the social skills of your teen since he/she will be in the midst of so many people. Bowling or skating while others watch will help to burst their bubble, or help your teen find new things which they are exceptionally good at!

ACTIVITIES FOR KINDERGARTEN:

Your child needs the right guidance for behaviour and good communication. The following social activities are excellent ways to improve social skills in kindergarten and pre-schoolers during their developmental stages.

21. Eye on the Forehead

Materials Needed: Eye stickers

How To: Separate the kids into different pairs. Then place an eye sticker on the forehead of one teammate. Encourage the other teammate to look closely at the label without blinking. The round ends when the player blinks. Then swap the position of teammates and repeat the game. This game will train your kindergarten to look in the right direction without feeling intimidated. The game is a fun social skill activity for kindergarten.

22. Building Vocabulary

Materials Needed: Objects like a toy or a kitchen tool.

How To: Give a child an object and ask her to describe what she feels about the object from her perspective. The trick is to make the object into something different from what it is. For instance, an empty cup can be described as a party hat. This game aims to develop story building and vocabulary skills in kids. Make sure you demonstrate first to help your child get the idea of the game.

23. Setting the Table

Materials Needed: Scissors, markers, construction paper in 7 colours and double-sided tape.

How To: Layout the table for your toddler to watch and learn. Now, encourage your kid to draw the following on the construction paper, and then cut them out.

- Dinner fork
- Salad fork
- Plate
- Water glass
- Napkin
- Soupspoon
- Teaspoon
- Knife

This game will help your child feel as though he or she is helping you with a "grown-up" activity like setting the table, thereby promoting creativity with household objects.

24. Mimic Me

This social skill activity is designed for babies.

How To: As the name implies, the trick of the game is to get the kids to mimic you. Touch your forehead and encourage your kid to do so. If you touch your nose, encourage him/her to do the same. Lightly box your ears and encourage them to do the same. The Mimic Me activity will help your kid pick up expressions and allow them to read social cues through mimicking.

25. Space Invader

Materials Needed: Picture of cartoon aliens, Popsicle sticks, glue, and crayons.

How To: Ask your child to colour the alien cartoon images, then cut it out. Stick the pictures of the aliens to the Popsicle sticks. While attaching the images, explain to your kid that it's essential to respect the personal space of others. Also, you can teach the child to use gentle hands to get the attention of someone rather than shouting or hitting the person.

Furthermore, explain to him that you are the alien he coloured while he's the space invader. When he is putting up his mark of the space invader, you as an alien would need time to regroup. Allow him time to regroup too. This way, you can teach him the concept of giving people the space to play on their own.

26. One Question Interview

Materials Needed: Pen, cards.

How To: On the cards, jot simple questions such as, "What's your favourite pet? What's your favourite food?" Have the kids form a circle while sitting. Now pass the cards around and instruct each person to read the question aloud. Send the kids to another room and form pairs in five minutes. When they come back, make them ask each other the questions and listen to the answers. Ask each kid individually what he/she learned from the partner. This activity aims to encourage active listening skills in children and helps them to know each other better.

27. Telephone Skills

Materials Needed: Scissors, card stock paper, small sticky notes.

How To: Instruct your child to use the card stock paper to model a telephone. Draw a rectangular shape on the card stock and cut it out. Use the rectangular shape to replicate the keys of the phone by sticking the round number stickers. Now give the child your number and encourage him to practice dialling and calling. You can also teach him emergency numbers.

When your kid dials your number from the telephone, pick your phone and talk to him. Engage him just like you'd engage any other adult. This activity will help to teach your kid communication skills and how to interact with others on the phone. You can also encourage them to make different kinds of phones… like what an alien might use to talk to his family… to inspire creativity.

28. Swinging

Take your child to a community park close to you for swinging. Make sure to make eye contact with him while he's swinging back and forth. If you are standing to his right, tell him to reach for you using his right foot and if you are standing on his left, tell him to use his left foot to contact you. This swinging activity will help to shift his focus to you and make him calm. Kids enjoy swinging; thus, it is often a favourite social activity for children.

29. Freeze It

This is a great social skill activity for teens and high school students to enhance their team-building skills.

How To: Gather the kids in the garden or the hall room. Choose a 'Tagger', and ask the others to form a horizontal line. Then ask the kids to freeze like statues with no sound or movement. Now, the 'Tagger' will make every effort to get the other kids to laugh and the first kid to laugh will be made the 'Tagger' for the next round. The freeze

'Tagger' social skill activity teaches kids patience and self-control, which happen to be critical social skills, as well as having a wonderful time with their classmates!

30. Manners and More

Social skills activities for students in preschools help to enhance their personal growth and development. Manners and More is one of such activity.

Materials Needed: Magazine, construction paper, scissors, glue, colours and markers.

How To: To start with, talk to the children about good and bad manners. Inform them that the difference between good and bad behaviour is a thin line. For instance, greeting people respectfully with eye contact, or saying "please and thank you". Tell the kids to create a collage on good and bad manners using the magazine cut-out. You can even spice it up by requesting them to make a slogan with styles.

31. Word Strips

Materials Needed: Pen, paper, double-sided tape.

How To: Draw and cut out words like hygiene, neat, clean, peace, and silence. Now talk to the child about the essential rules like maintaining silence while in the library, keeping a low tone when someone is making a call, keeping the closet clean and so on. Write the essential rules on a strip and cut it out. Then ask your child to stick the words on the appropriate strip. This will show your children the importance of specific actions and help remind them how to be more courteous, respectful young adults.

32. Name Game

Material Needed: A ball

How To: Make the kids form a circle while seated and give one of them a ball. Ask the kid holding the ball to pick a fellow player, give him a name and pass the ball to him. The fellow player will in turn choose another player, name him and pass the ball to him. This entertaining activity will allow your children to create friendships with one another as it helps their social skills.

As a parent or teacher, there are so many things you can do to improve the social skills of your children. All you need do is plan the appropriate activities that will motivate your child/teen; then in no time, you will come to see significant improvement in your child's sociability, and your once shy teen will evolve into a confident young adult.

3

DEVELOPING HEALTHY SELF-ESTEEM

SELF-ESTEEM is an essential key to success in life. A healthy self-esteem or a positive self-concept is necessary for the success and happiness of children and teenagers. This section talks about the basics that parents and teachers can adapt to help their kids and teens improve their self-esteem.

Simply defined, self-esteem is a measure of how we feel about ourselves, and these feelings are impacted by the behaviours we exhibit. For instance, a child or teenager who has high self-esteem will find it easy to:

- Take responsibility
- Handle frustration
- Act without depending on anyone
- Talk of his/her accomplishments respectfully
- Take on new challenges and tasks confidently
- Handle negative and positive emotions
- Provide help for others

A young girl was being bullied in school because of her looks. The children made fun of her hair and the clothes she wore. No one asked why she wore such clothes to school and no one cared enough about how she felt when awkward remarks were made about her clothing options. There was a rumour claiming she showers once a week and ate till she passed out. However unrealistic this may be, people still laughed and made fun of her.

Being a teenager in upper school is hard enough with the stereotypes, class segregation and intimidation. Unfortunately, these are some of the significant events that can lead to depression. Another is when you feel like you don't have a lot of friends or none at all to have your back through the hard times. This beautiful young girl would often bawl her eyes out before attending lectures for that day and later return home feeling low.

On a particular day of being verbally abused she ran into her gym teacher who shared her high school experience; she talked for long hours like she was expressing someone else's story.

"Did it ever get better?" she asked inquisitively at the end of her teacher's story,

"YES," the teacher said vibrantly. 'Know your worth, and do not in any way let anyone put you down. '

The words echoed in her ears till she laid her head on the soft pillow to sleep as she muttered: "I know my worth. "

She walked down the hall gleefully the next day ignoring the comments from people. Eyes drifted slowly as she walked by. Her teacher reached out to her mum, and with the help of her teacher, her grades got better and her mum always reminded her of her self-worth and how undeniably confident she ought to be.

She finally graduated from school with a high GPA and gained admission into five prospective universities. That simple conversation with her gym teacher helped that young girl change her life for the better.

On the flip side, a child with low self-esteem will be shy and struggle to try new things and adventures, feel unwanted and unloved, and begin to blame others for his/her shortcomings. They will pretend to feel different emotionally; and in most cases, if the child feels different emotionally, they will find it challenging to handle a usual dose of frustration, put down their abilities and talents, and be easily swayed by peer pressure. Low self-esteem becomes a self-fulfilling prophecy where your child feels worse and worse because of their continual lack of self-worth.

More than anyone else, parents are best suited to build the self-esteem of their children and teens. Building the self-esteem of children and teens isn't a difficult thing to do. What most parents do not know is that their actions and words have an impact on their kids, and go a long way to impact their feelings.

Here are some ways to build self-esteem in your kids:

Teach your child the importance and the sense of empowerment that can be felt from loving himself/herself. "The development of healthy or positive self-esteem is significant to the happiness and success of children" [1]. As the source states, happiness and success are just two of the factors that can only be achieved if a person, not only a child, has a sense of love for themselves. Being happy in their own skin and with who they are in terms of personality and the choices they make is crucial to a positive development as they age and grow.

Parental attitudes and behaviour heavily affect the development of self-esteem in young children, so the majority of this rests on you. Avoid the assumption that a child will automatically love themselves. It's simply not the case and it will never work like that. Children are ever-developing and love for oneself can be a challenging thing to grapple with. Ever developing and ever-changing, the parameters are much different and a child needs that reassurance, particularly if they already have areas of concern when it comes to their self-esteem.

The minute your child begins to compare themselves to others is the minute action must be taken. Positive behaviours and mindsets should be instilled in your child, guiding them to not focus on what they believe to be negatives but instilling a sense of strength and giving them the freedom to recognise their strengths, without directly approaching the subject.

Negativity must be discouraged, especially in regards to spreading rumours and speaking negatively of others. This is something you will often hear stories of in the playground. As a child, I recall one of my friends being called "Fat" for the first time. Until that point, he wasn't even aware that he was technically overweight according to the BMI scale - he was only four years old, so he had no reason to be thinking about this, he should have had a carefree attitude. Upon hearing this, he began to worry about his weight, something he should have never considered at such a young age.

It's therefore essential to control these behaviours, prevent them and encourage your child to avoid partaking in such negative practices that can be destructive and debilitating for other children. "Identify and redirect your children's inaccurate beliefs. Teach them how to think in positive ways, and change their negative thoughts about themselves to positive ones" [1]. Though the quotation above only refers to the child themselves, these behaviours should be applied to how they socialise with other children.

Those who focus on the weaknesses of others or the inadequacies of their own appear to struggle with their further development and careers in later life. Negativity is a breeding ground for failure. Instil positivity and give a child the foundations for happiness, freedom and future success.

Odd behaviours, particularly between the ages of 8-11 years should be noted. Allow them room to grow and learn while ensuring they understand that their frustrations, if that's how they are feeling, should not cause others any pain. Their negativity should not be transferred, it should be rectified with a positive environment for learning and recreation.

Your child will inevitably change as years go by; they'll get taller, they'll get stronger but one thing should always remain the same; their core values. It's vital that without commanding it, you instil the belief system that core values do not change. They are not up for negotiation and they are crucial to becoming positive members of society with high chances for success.

33. Mention it to your son/daughter when he/she does something to impress you.

Parents and teachers are often too quick to express negative feelings to children, but do not get around to expressing positive feelings as often. When your child does something to impress you and you feel right about him/her, mention it. A child doesn't know that you are excited and feeling right about him/her until you say it to them. Your child wants to hear you say, "Oh, I like having you in the family. " Children do not forget the positive feelings we express to them; they keep these positive feelings in a storehouse to replay them over and over again when they are feeling low. Your words of encouragement help your teenager brush off the struggles they may be facing outside of your home. Form a habit of giving your child words of encouragement every day.

Billy and his mother went to the supermarket to get some groceries. Then Billy went ahead to have some fun with the children playing outside. One of the kids, a tiny girl began to chase her doll that fell and was rolling into a nearby pit. Billy ran ahead of her in a swift and got the toy just as it was rolling inside. It was so dramatic. The little girl, who was so ecstatic, thanked Billy and went into the supermarket to tell her mum. Billy's mum overhead what the little girl was telling her mum and she just had to follow them to see the hero boy.

Stepping out and seeing a crowd hovering over her son, she asked the little girl: Who did you say saved your doll? The little girl pointed to Billy and said, "He's the one."

Today, Billy is a firefighter, and when he was asked what motivated him to that, he said, "I most likely will never forget that day I saved that girl's doll. My mum looked at me and said, 'I've always known you are a hero. But I thought you were only my hero. I now know you are really going to save lives.'"

Whenever Billy feels weary, he thinks of his mum and how much she values him. That's what you get when you say positive things to your child when they impress you. You never know; you might be putting something in their future.

The values taught to children between the ages of three and seven remain with them for the rest of their life. It's therefore crucial to paint the right kind of picture within their minds, setting them up for later life. This isn't to say you should show them the harsh realities of the overcrowded marketplace or just how competitive the job market of today is, rather it means you should instil in them the positivity and values needed to survive in that world. Instead of focusing on the negatives.

One way you can do this is by ensuring your child has the right view of who they are, telling them the qualities they have and praising them when they do something good. "Getting positive but realistic feedback helps them to build their self-esteem based on real skills and strengths" [2].

34. Be generous with praise.

Appreciate your child when he's excelling at a task. You must develop the habit of looking for situations where your child is displaying an actual practice or doing a good job.

Whenever your child finishes a task, you could say, "I really like how you handled the task" or "I like how you arranged your room". When you observe your child or teen coming up with a new talent or learning how to play a new instrument, you should appreciate him/her for making an effort, and telling him how well he played. Irrespective of where you are, be it outside or inside, with friends or family, do not hesitate to shower your child with praises. That way, your child will feel loved and wanted.

Also, you can praise your teen by pointing out positive character traits. For example, "You are a brilliant person. . . I like the way you don't take no for an answer. " Some parents think that showering their child/children with praise in excess makes the child want to go haywire or misbehave. But it simply helps your child understand his/her self-worth.

May I add: there is nothing like excessive praise. Showering praise on your child makes the child do the exact opposite of misbehaving. For example, your child made a beautiful drawing and came to show it to you and you responded with something like, "Oh, my love! Sharon, did you really draw this? Oh, sweetheart! It is stunning. How did you come about this? I will really love to have it pasted in my room. Let's say these colours are just as bright as you. You know what? I can feel myself blushing already!"

Just imagine yourself as a child being showered with such praise. I tell you, that's exactly how your child would feel. Praise specific aspects of work done; e. g. "You polished your shoes properly," or praise the child for being creative at a given task. If you appreciate the child often and generally, the child might think that he/she is already good enough whereas it is only in one aspect that is graded good, giving room for improvement as well. Positive reinforcement for tasks that you deem essential will encourage your child to continue to do them, and grow into a better-rounded individual.

It is only when we appreciate our children's efforts that we lay a foundation for constructive criticism; otherwise, you will only be hurling bricks at them. You cannot write with chalk/board marker on the thin air; you need a whiteboard if children are to see what you are writing. Even so, expressed appreciation forms the board on which we can write and speak the truth in love to our kids. As part of appreciation, send them parcels, when coming from outside, to give a pleasant surprise. Say, "Daddy to son," or "mum to son".

35. Teach your son/daughter to develop the habit of making positive declarations and self-statements.

Self-statements are very important in every action we take and in everything we do. Psychologists have discovered that negative self-statement is one of the main drivers of anxiety and depression. The thoughts that run through our mind determine how we feel; and our feelings, in turn, drive our behaviour. As such, it's crucial to teach your teens to use positive self-statements.

Here are some examples of positive self-statements:

- I'll find a solution to this problem if I keep on trying.
- There's no problem should our team lose today. We put in the best efforts and we can't win every day.
- I feel good when I help others even though they do not notice or show appreciation.

For example, your child had a competition and lost to his opponent. He came home feeling frustrated and started saying: "I am a loser, dad. I lost to Ken, and it's just so awful."

As a parent, you shouldn't accept that from him. You should respond with something like, "Matt! I have always told you, you are not a loser. The day you begin to see yourself as a loser, you become one. You might lose to him today but let's just say you are way better than him in other things and you will always be my winner. " You should pay close attention to your child's expression after this. You'll realise sooner that positive declarations go a long way. Habits are your actions that determine your destiny.

36. Steer away from criticisms that take the form of shame or ridicule.

No law forbids you from criticising your child when necessary; it's an appropriate thing to do. However, it results in shame or ridicule when you express criticism directly to your child. It's imperative that you learn how best to use the "I-statements" rather than the "You-statements" when expressing criticism.

For instance, instead of saying, "Why are you so lazy and rough," to your child when his/her closet is untidy, consider saying, "I would like for you to tidy up your closet. " This removes the blame from your child, and removes the accusatory tone. They will relate with the "You-statement. "

37. Teach your child how to make and recognise the right decisions.

Children are not aware that they make decisions even though they make decisions quite often. There are many ways carers, teachers and parents can help children improve their ability to make the right decisions consciously:

- Help your child identify the problem that calls for the decision.
- Ask questions that target what they think about the situation and what they want to change about the situation.
- Talk about the possible solutions to the problem. A

problem usually has more than one answer, so you should point this out and suggest alternatives in the event where your child can only think of one solution.

- Let the child choose a solution only after he/she has thought about all solutions and weighed their consequences. Note that the best solution should be the one that will resolve the problem and at the same time make the child happy, while still considering the feelings of those around them.
- Then, evaluate the results of the solution with the child. Did the solution resolve the problem? Did it fail? If yes, why?

Go over the tactics again with your child. This will help the child make the right decision the next time he has to make one.

Molly, a ten-year-old kid, had the opportunity of going to either a cinema or a museum. After a while, she decided on going to the cinema. Her mum asked her why? She said because she's going to have fun watching movies. Read their conversation:

Mother: Don't you think you will have much fun in the museum?

Daughter: I don't know. There will be no movies.

Mother: Do you only have fun watching movies?

Daughter: Well, no.

Mother: You always told me you liked history, yeah?

Daughter: Yes, I love history.

Mother: Don't you think going to the museum will give you more knowledge? And trust me, it's always fun.

Daughter: Really? (Smiles)

Mother: Yes of course. It's better than going to the cinema. You are just going to watch fiction movies there; but the museum, it is real, baby.

Daughter: Wow! I am going to the museum.

Mother: Not the cinema again?

Daughter: No mum.

Mother: Why?

Daughter: Because I am not going to gain more knowledge in the cinema.

Mother: All right, baby. Good of you.

You just read that right?

Imagine the mum just telling Molly she can't go to the cinema. Molly would be forced to go to the museum but will not be happy at all. Helping the children make decisions and letting them know the results of the decision can pay dividends later in life.

Teens want you to believe in them. Before you challenge your teen to change his or her choices, give them the understanding that you believe in them, hug and assure them that you believe in them. Tell them why you do not agree with them on a matter. That's trust, that's faith.

Particularly in the digital age of today where peer pressure is at an all-time high and social media is just an extension of playground behaviours, it's essential to see things from their perspective. Put yourself in their shoes and see how they may want to make their own choices because 'Sarah has Instagram' and 'Jo has done it so why can't I?'. With social media, that fear of missing out has only been made more significant and further given it the spotlight.

"Social media can easily affect the kids, the reason is sometimes people shares photos, videos on media that contain violence and negative things which can affect the behaviour of kids or teenagers" [3]. Though violence doesn't apply in this context, negativity and aspects of social media that can have a negative effect on your teenager can further strengthen the divide between you and your teenager. Bridge that gap and give them the confidence that they need to know you trust them but want them to make the right decision, so hope that they will. If they think you don't care, they'll have the freedom to do as they please. If they think you care but will give them space to evaluate the choice themselves, it shows them that you care and they'll likely see things from the perspective you were hoping for.

Show understanding instead of being suspicious. This makes teens to trust you and makes them happy. It is tough not to be suspicious of teenagers because they do what we do not understand. But don't let them know you are suspicious. When they are relaxed you can explain to them your concerns. They want you to respect their choices and desires. "Parenting involves allowing our children to have more responsibilities and freedoms as they grow older. Generally speaking, the goal is to let go, and letting go requires trust" [4].

38. Provide structure for your kid by developing a positive approach.

Kids and teens are expected to take responsibility for their actions and behaviour. Kids and teens should learn self-discipline. To do this, the onus is on the parent to take up the role of a teacher or coach rather than of a punisher and disciplinarian. The next ten tips are ways to help your child develop high self-esteem through self-discipline and becoming a more responsible individual.

We are to teach kids about taking responsibility for themselves, for people around them, for the world around them, for their family, country and for their purpose, goals and passion.

39. Teach your child to change his/her demands to preferences.

Teach your child and teen that he/she will not always get what he wants, so there's no cause to be angry. Set a good example to inspire your child against getting angry unnecessarily when they do not understand precisely what they want. Also, encourage your child when she expresses appropriate irritation when necessary rather than anger. You are not mostly going to be smiling to your child each time he or she has a need.

Let the child know that some needs are best not met at the moment. Expressing displeasure is okay, but getting angry and keeping malice are inappropriate behaviours.

40. Encourage children to request for the things they want with confidence, but with no guarantee the request will always be granted.

Encourage your children to ask what they desire. If your child finds it very difficult to walk up to you and request something, then you should check and make sure you are open and accommodating to accept their needs and let them know that they could always ask you anything they want. That isn't a guarantee that they will still get everything they ask. But approaching you is an assurance that they could get what they want.

What they ask may be delayed, but their asking helps you to know their line of thought. Children who grow up having all they want have no values for things, and when they grow up they get easily frustrated because they cannot work hard enough for what they want.

Children cannot have it because they want it. Help them overcome instant gratification so that they can work hard and get fulfilment. Parents have to work hard at this, as helping your child find the perfect balance between asking for what they need, and working hard for the things they deem necessary to them can be a difficult task to achieve.

41. Teach children that they are creators and responsible for the feelings they experience.

Your children need to know that they are responsible for their emotions and feelings. However, they aren't accountable for how others feel. Abstain from taking out your feelings on your children, but encourage them to reach out to you with emotions they are having.

42. Stir your child to develop interests and hobbies they find pleasurable and can pursue without having to depend on anyone.

Did you find that your child enjoys watching sports on TV? Encourage him/her to join the school's sports team. Your child will enjoy changing what she sees on TV into reality. Mind you, TV watching might lead to a future career. And if you noticed your child loves reading fiction books and magazines; then encourage him/her by buying books they'd like to read. You never know, you might be investing in a great future writer.

Reading books, even fairy tales, could be useful, and parents should discuss the book the child has read. Written language is one of the supreme achievements of human beings. It has enabled our ability to communicate over distances, to record history to analyse at new depths, and to create new artistic forms. It is a cultural invention that in turn has had profound cultural and social effects" [5].

A child's first experience of the world is through the words of someone else's dream. Parents should provide further explanation and insight to young children the images or characters they read about. For instance, a child reading about Cinderella might feel they will live happily after, but as a fairy tale, Cinderella is not real. But this is not the same as the story of David and Goliath, which was a true story, and a child, though small now, can look forward to doing great things, overcoming significant challenges. Bible stories are more real than Jacklin Wilsons books (story of Tracey Beaker) or Best Friends Storm Breaker by Anthony Horowitz which children tend to believe, and miss their expectations.

Stories like Tracey Beaker in particular have provided children with the perspective of an 'unloved' child, a polar opposite to what most of us experienced as children. It's an entirely new perspective and therefore is an opportunity for learning what it would be like for a child in care. Though it's not real, it's educational in many ways.

Make sure the stories are valid so that your children don't have a fake foundation that could mess them up when they are older. Some think that breakfast must be served in bed every time. But that is not the reality of real life.

43. Leave children to settle their disputes with friends and siblings.

Encourage children to settle disputes and conflicts with friends or siblings (This will be covered in Chapter 5). Do not interfere except when necessary. Resolving disputes and conflicts on their own will further boost their self-esteem, and help let them figure out on their own a right way or method on how to handle difficult situations.

44. Teach children 'tease tolerance' and point out that some teasing does not hurt.

Children should learn to use positive self-statements to cope with teasing and to ignore it. Whenever your child is being teased, teach him/her to resolve within, or say something like: "nicknames cannot hurt me. . . I'm stronger than teases. . . If I can ignore this tease, I'll build emotional muscle. "

45. Teach children to rely on their strengths by identifying all the things they are capable of.

This of course doesn't mean children should become bullies and use their strengths negatively on others. Relying on their strengths is a straightforward way of knowing how much they love themselves and trust so much in their abilities and capabilities. Building on their strengths effectively allows them to continue to grow these strengths and add to their self-esteem. If from a tender age a child is made to discover the importance of his/her abilities, develop their capabilities and rely on their strength, the parents have done well.

We are all to work on our flaws, weaknesses and strengths throughout life, it's part of what makes us human. We have an inbuilt desire for development, which first starts with self-evaluation.

Sometimes however, no matter how you work on your weaknesses, they may never turn into your strengths. But recognising them and allowing children to identify their current strengths is a whole other situation. Finding out who you are and who your child is, is a helpful start, this is why some things are hard for some and more comfortable for others. One activity that has proved useful for parents and children alike is to create a 'strengths chain', it's a crafty way of encouraging children (parents should join in and do their own too) [6]. This allows them to realise what they're really capable of while utilising and developing their arts and crafts skills too. Paper chains look good also, so that's a bonus.

In recognising their strengths, children must also learn to utilise their skills and operate in different environments with different personality types. Rather than thinking "Why can't I be like that; why am I not good at that?" your child should be encouraged to focus on the things that they can do that others can't. This ideology should follow them through later life.

46. Encourage children to treat peers and siblings precisely the way they would want to be treated.

Sometimes, children act so bizarrely and weird you begin to wonder what they were thinking and why they do what they do. For example, Michael was playing ball in the garden while his little sister, Ellen, was playing with her doll. When Ellen got in Michael's way, Michael got angry and threw the toy away. The mother rushed to the garden when she heard Ellen's cry. The conversation below ensued:

Mother: Why did you throw her doll away, Michael?

Michael: She got in my way, mum. I was playing my ball.

Mother: Do you know your sister really liked that doll?

Michael: Yes, mum.

Mother: Do you like your ball?

Michael: Yes, mum.

Mother: Would you like me to throw your ball over the garden just like you did to Ellen's doll?

Michael: No, mum. I am sorry.

Mother: Would sorry change anything?

Michael: No, mum.

Mother: So what did you learn?

Michael: Never to hurt people with what they value.

Mother: Plus whatever you do to anyone would be done back to you by someone else. Got that?

Michael: Yes, mum.

And that's it. Let children know that whatever they do to anyone would be done back to them. They ought to treat people the way they would want to be treated. This is an essential lesson to instil in children and growing teenagers to help them maintain good relationships as they continue to grow.

47. Help children learn that there are several possibilities and alternatives instead of depending on just one option for satisfaction.

A child who is friends with just one person will become friendless when the friend moves away or when he/she loses the friend. On the flip side, a child who has several people as friends will still have many friends if and whenever he/she loses one. This principle of friends also applies to several areas. Whenever you limit yourself to one means of satisfaction, you reduce your potential for getting satisfied. So, when you teach your children that there are several alternatives and possibilities in every situation, you increase their potential for getting happy.

You can do this by inspiring your children to increase their outreach in activities, and provide them with outlets where they get to be with a lot of different people at once.

48. Teach your son/daughter not to take themselves too seriously by laughing with them, and encouraging them to laugh at themselves.

Having a great sense of humour as well as the ability to take life lightly are the essential keys to increasing one's overall fun. It all depends on you, though. If you, as a parent, never have the time to sit, laugh and have fun with your kids, they might never see the reason to do that as well. Make them laugh by cracking jokes with them. It's great fun! All by themselves, they will come to learn laughter as a crucial means for enjoying life.

It's all well known that children, ages 15-17 tend to argue more, get irritated more, get moody; and all that because their body changes as they transit from childhood into adolescence. It is not a fault of theirs, and everyone goes through this stage in life. At this stage, take a walk with them to the park and explain to them why this is happening. Teach them to try to control their tendencies at this period and learn to cope with the changes in their body. "It may be helpful to know that the conflict most parents endure during their child's teen years usually subsides by the age of 16" [7]. If you can make it any clearer to them that how they are feeling is entirely reasonable and a part of the transition process, it would be beneficial to their overall self-esteem and development.

They must know the changes aren't because they are misbehaving; if they are left to think they're the root cause of how they feel and it's not a natural process, they will only get angrier, disagree more and further force their opinions to be heard.

It can cause feelings of depression in the teenager, where they may wither, go back into their shell and regress as a means of avoiding conflict and making the situation worse. "The teen years can be extremely tough and depression affects teenagers far more often than many of us realise. In fact, it's estimated that one in five adolescents from all walks of life will suffer from depression at some point during their teen years. However, while depression is highly treatable, most depressed teens never receive help" [8]

As parents, we should aim to prevent this regression by creating more positive time spent with our children, particularly teenagers. Showing softness in love, joking around with our children and helping them to relax by encouraging them to dedicate more time to family and recreational time, away from social media, digital devices and negativity that can only make the transition to adolescence worse.

Agree with your child more, ask them to do things through suggestions, have more patience, and don't be irritated you ask them to do stuff and it took them an hour to do what could be completed in no more than five minutes. When parents panic at this stage, they make things more difficult. Rather, laugh over it. Share a joke or two over it. They will overcome it. Always know that your children are not having this experience alone; you are in it with them. "The journey through these years is easier when parents, families and care-givers learn as much as they can about this time in children's lives and when they give their children support" [9].

Yes, children of this age don't always want to be around you. Respect that. They don't want to be seen by their friends with you. Take that; they will get over it. Don't ban or provoke them. Instead, support and prevent them from being rude or do unlawful things. By speaking to just one parent with a teenager, the first line from them was "He never wants to spend time with me. He's always out with his friends. When he is in the house, he's on his Xbox". Though it appears negative on the face of it, it's not unlike any other parent-adolescent relationship.

At this age children want to experiment with many things, they're developing a greater sense of who they are and who they want to be. Compliment their efforts in discovering who they are and the journey they're taking, rather than discouraging it or saying they're going wrong. Yes, their looks and mood swing tend to make them rude. Yet be supportive to them in their imperfection, close your eyes to many things that are not erring.

Children at this age appreciate truthfulness and sincerity providing it's coming from a good place, not criticising the person they want to be or who they want to spend time with.

They don't want to see you use your experience to say you know it all. They don't want hypocrisy. The first thing a child will reply to you is "Well you did it when you were younger" or something to that degree, they always do and always will. They're right too. So, admit your faults before them so they don't see you as perfect and they are not perfect. They want to relate more with their friends, read newspapers, magazines and books which influence them, and look down on your advice. Yet, if you approach them as a friend, they will not look down on you.

Don't be surprised that children during this age period enjoy more freedom with their friends and like to do stuff with people of their age. Make sure they are not afraid of you, but can bring their friends home. Yes, they tend to be more stubborn, resolute, stronger to argue and affirm their rightness and why you are wrong. When the child is vehement and wants to prove he or she is stronger, you step back so you don't lose him/her as he/she is still looking to find out who they really are. It's an important journey. "Growing up is more than the physical changes that occur, such as getting taller or more muscular. This passage is a time for establishing independence, testing limits, trying on different roles, exploring new feelings, and fostering intellectual growth" [10].

Also at this stage, the child tends to experiment with looks. Use respect and honour, use jokes and laughing, which all can make him think that you understand him/her better - proving it's not entirely at their expense and everybody involved is having fun. One parent once shared a story of how her father, the child's grandfather had once referred the child as 'pizza face' in a very jokingly fashion, referring to her blackhead breakout, believing she saw it as the joke it was supposed to be. She didn't.

Be as relatable as possible and make things as fun as possible at home but also pick up on the more serious, underlying issues, if there are any. Share their hurts and concerns. Some are rebellious because no one paid attention to them. They worry about how they look, more introverted because the body is going through hormonal changes. Tell them to expect and entertain the experience. Tell about your experience and failures. Don't give your children false hope; they are sensitive to false hope.

Anything you are doing wrong puts them away and makes them listen to other people apart from you. So, be sincere and real. Come to their level and be no hypocrite. Don't correct them publicly. Express more patience, and don't try to crucify them for every infraction. Laugh over matters and chat rather than give teachings and express a discussion on every trivial matter. It's important however to remember that, especially if you're a first-time parent, you're undergoing a learning process of how to deal with an ever-changing, ever-growing adolescent just like they're learning how to deal with being one. Mistakes are going to happen, but as long as they know it's normal and natural, it will make things as easy as possible.

With children of this age, live more like brothers and sisters, and listen to them more. Hear their inner cry that says, "Mum, trust me; give me the freedom that allows me to explore things. " Don't give them false hope. They don't see themselves as kids; so don't see them like that. Relate with them as grown-ups.

4

EMPATHY SKILLS

Truth be told, teenagers are famous for being self-involved and self-centred. We have come to the age where the world doesn't matter much to teenagers, and this has resulted in lack of empathy. It's no surprise that parents and teachers now feel that they are fighting a battle that seems lost already – a battle against the most self-centred generation, a generation which strives to meet the needs of themselves before wanting to help those around them.

We all see how self-centeredness has become the music of this generation. According to renowned psychologist Dr Nathan DeWall, this generation teenagers are completely obsessed and in love with themselves, and nothing backs this fact more than the hostile turn and obsession with self-ego heard in the popular music of today. His theory stems from the frequent use of "I" and "me" words followed closely by anger-related words which describe various life situations. There is an apparent decline in the use of "us" and "we" in lyrics and the use of positive emotions.

The onus is now on parents and teachers to teach teenagers empathy and help them see beyond their selfish desires. This urges the question: How can we teach teenagers to continue to look outside of the realm of what their needs are?

To start, we need to show them what empathy is and how it can make them better and propelled to live a great life. Even as a parent or teacher, you want your teens and students to be empathetic to you. So, the sooner you introduce them to empathy, the better for you and them.

Another reason why it's expedient for you to teach your pre-teen and teenagers empathy is that empathy is the bedrock of all positive emotions. Hence, understanding it is necessary for social and bonding skills. Here are some ways to teach your teens empathy:

49. "Do Unto Others. . . . "

Here is a paraphrase of a statement credited to Jesus Christ, the greatest Teacher of all time: "Do to others what you expect them to do to you. " Teens who have emotional needs that aren't attended to will find it uneasy to understand the emotional needs of people around them. As a parent embarking on the journey of teaching your teen empathy and how to interpret the emotions and needs of others, you must first understand their own. Trust their decisions and be supportive. You need to accept and understand their needs and passion to be able to help them understand the concept of empathy.

It's important to highlight the importance of showing empathy and treating other people with the same level of decency that they would wish to be shown. Whether you have a good day or bad day, you show the same kindness and respect. Save them from making a colossal mistake and potentially upsetting them, show them the benefits of being a kind, respectful member of society. This is particularly important in the digital age of today where social media is rife with internet trolls and is a breeding ground for negativity. It's essential for your child not to get sucked into that.

50. Never compare your teen with yourself or others.

You need to understand that your teen is a person with his own right; so never compare him/her with yourself. The fact that you can comprehend, understand and relate well with others doesn't mean that your teen will automatically have the ability too. You learnt it, remember? Do not work against your teenager, otherwise they will become alienated and all efforts to teach them empathy will prove abortive. Work with your teenager to help see that through comparing themselves to others, they do not achieve the empathy which you are striving to instil in them. As mentioned earlier, it's very easy for children to compare themselves to others, much like many of us do as adults with our peers, be it colleagues or friends. Rather than allowing for this behaviour, though it is reasonable and natural, attempt to subdue it somewhat, teach them to appreciate what they have and make the most of it.

Depending on your stand we can simply teach that life doesn't always go the way we want it to and this is an opportunity to learn that.

The point is, we have all been raised differently, will experience different things, have different skillsets and own various possessions. Show your child this side of life and teach them to be what they want to be.

"Look at Emma, Mrs Benson's daughter. She is going to medical school next year and look at you, you've been out of high school since the last two years and you've found nothing good to do with your life. "

This sort of statement shouldn't come out of the mouth of a parent. If your daughter, as you said, hasn't found something to do with her life, do you sit down and start comparing her with Emma, Mrs Benson's daughter? Many parents are disappointed in children, who they never taught. You should be reacting to issues with positive language, not negative words like this one. When you overreact to a child's failure or disappointments, they do the same. They may over-react openly in a violent manner or inwardly in a depressed way. None of that is good. "Parents love their children and want the best for them. However, children don't come with directions and don't always respond or behave the way you want them to" [11]. Approach every subject with care, speak to them in a positive manner, because you really don't know the kind of response you'll get with the safest, most positive of messages sometimes.

In the house, be the teacher you should be. Honour and respect your child. Every child must be respected. Some parents are proud of their children in front of other people and not in front of the child himself. It has to be both ways. Praising the child in public but condemning her at home won't help a tiny bit. You are just giving more room to justify a rebellious attitude from your daughter.

Why don't you sit her down and ask her how she views life and her present situation. Try to know what is going on in her mind. She might just be craving to talk to you. Comparing your teen with another teen is a wrong approach. Not only does it force the child to compare herself to others continuously, it also stops the child from creating positive self-worth, which will help her grow in the long run.

51. Be a great model.

Children are copycats, and copy whatever they see their parents doing. By being a great role model and demonstrating emotions such as empathy and sympathy yourself, you can help your teen know the importance of empathy. You certainly cannot teach your teen what you don't practice. When you show sympathy to those around you and your children can see that, it becomes part of them. Children remember what you do, not what you teach. We can all be servant leaders at home, not a boss.

52. Experience the pain.

We find it much easier to relate with people we perceive to be similar to us. So, teach your teen the similarities they have with other people. You can start with yourself. Share your daily experiences; share your emotions and how you handle your feelings. Show just how much you and your teen have in common; then in turn, they will begin to empathise with you more often.

Sometimes, a teenager comes against a wall emotionally, and thinks she is the only one having the emotion and experience. Demonstrate that you have passed through the stage yourself and know what it is. The moment your teenager can recognise their emotions and master how you deal with emotions, he/she begins to find it easy to adopt the same approach when dealing with their own feelings.

The listed approaches to developing empathy skills are just a few ways to turn the self-centred teen into one that is self-aware of others. Still, the best way to teach children and teen empathy is to show them what empathy is by understanding their feelings and needs, and acknowledging that others exist. Encouraging them to put themselves in other's shoes to see what they are going through. Kids must know that there are different people in life, some short, ugly, fat etc. Every human deserves to be loved and respected.

To deliberately teach your child to have empathy and sympathy for people, one of the highest values in life is to feel the pain others feel. "Moral imagination is the capacity to empathise with others, i. e. , not just to feel for oneself, but to feel with and for others. This is something that education ought to cultivate and that citizens ought to bring to politics" [12].

One's got to live for something greater than oneself, ready to pay the price or bear some discomfort for the comfort of others. Until her death, Mother Theresa was renowned for pouring out her life to sacrifice for the good of others. That's a worthy example to follow.

5

CONFLICT RESOLUTION SKILLS

During adolescence, the time children spend with their peers becomes more significant than the time spent with parents and adults. Teens consider friendship very important and as they begin to pull away from their parents, they seek for the support and acceptance of their friends. Besides offering companionship, adolescent friendship helps to develop conflict resolution skills in teens and gives them stability during the transition, since they are friends with teens who like them and are also experiencing the same situations. Teens with good friends have high self-esteem and a high chance of academic achievement.

Truth be told, it's not easy to be a teenager. The time between teens and adulthood is full of both physical and emotional changes. With raging hormones, teenagers find it uneasy about being social. Sulking, temper tantrums and ignoring

parents are all peculiar to teenagers. Most teenagers feel like they are in a world of their own, that others do not get it, or understand how they think. Often time, the lack of empathy creates an environment where individuals feel like they are alone and have no one to turn to.

We've been there too, I'm glad to say. So we understand the feeling. Equipping your teen with the right skills set will help them to manage disorderly years better. Conflict resolution skills are part of the skills that all teenagers must learn.

How Prevalent Are Conflicts?

Conflict is part of life; it occurs all the time. No matter how you shield your child from friction, he/she has to face the reality of it. Conflict can happen anywhere, with friends, with siblings, with parents, and in the society at large. However, the one thing you should teach your teen is that conflict isn't a negative experience; it provides an opportunity to grow as an individual. Keep in mind that conflict can bring about needed change, a positive change at that.

Consequences Of Teenage Conflicts:

Without the appropriate skill set a teen can find himself/herself in tough situations as a result of conflicts. Even at home disputes that are not resolved can cause strained relationships in the family. Unresolved conflicts can bring about broken relationships, violence and hours of detention.

Consequences Of Teenage Conflicts:

Without the necessary skill set a teenager can land in tight situations due to conflicts. At home, unresolved conflicts can lead to strained relations with the ones they have come to hold dearest. Outside, it can lead to broken friendships, hours of detention, and even violence! Obviously, we want to teach our children how to handle these situations and de-escalate them effectively.

Teaching Teens Conflict Resolution Skills

The character of a child is forged by the values and principles they learn at school and the home. Therefore, it's safe to say that teachers and parents play a critical role in the mental and emotional development of children. You should teach your children when they are still young because it's challenging to change the behaviour of children once they progress into their teenage years.

When children progress into their teenage years, their bodies go through sudden and unexpected physical changes and they start to feel emotions that weren't felt before. Now, as they make efforts to cope with the new development, they turn into rebels, going against their teachers and parents. Their young mind tells them that their new-found changes mean they are now old enough to make decisions on their own, and our resistance to letting them make these critical choices can put an increased strain on the relationship we have been building with our child. During this time, teens experience many social conflicts.

As a parent, let it be a part of your assignment to help your child navigate life with as little setbacks as possible, and help them traverse the ones that they do experience. Start early and teach your teen conflict resolution skills. They may not know what you are doing for them today; in fact, they may not appreciate you today, but they are more likely to do so later. Meanwhile, you should laud yourself for a job well done.

CONFLICT RESOLUTION COMMANDMENTS

53. Conflict is a reality you cannot escape. Hiding from this reality will solve nothing.

Let your child know that conflicts and disputes are meant to happen, and will always occur; so there's no reason to hide from it. Conflict occurs to allow us to have a better understanding of ourselves. Many parents don't deem it necessary to tell their teens these things because they think the children on their own ought to learn. Laura and Lillian are best friends and have been friends since junior school. They are in high school and have just one year to finish. Laura noticed that Lillian always go through her phone, view her contacts and play games on her phone. Laura was okay with it until one day when she got to know that Lillian sent a provocative sexual message to a guy in their class through her phone. The conservation leaked and everyone thought it was Laura. Laura was hoping that Lillian would own up on it and excuse her (Laura) out of the whole mess, but she did not. Instead, Lillian was laughing with the other girls calling Laura names. Laura was deeply hurt and had the urge to go slap Lillian and kick some sense into her head but she felt it isn't right.

Three days later, Laura was still being friends with Lillian and never asked a thing about what had happened. Meanwhile, she was bottling a whole lot of rage inside of her, but felt unleashing her anger would result in a conflict which would be very wrong. She decided to keep the pain in her heart. After a few days, Laura's mum noticed Laura had not been eating well and seemed distant. After a lot of convincing words, she was forced to tell her mum what happened.

"So, you are scared to get angry at Lillian?" her mum queried, then explained. "But do you know that being irritated at what someone does to you isn't an example of a real bad feeling. It only shows that you are not completely satisfied with what the person said or did. It only shows you are human and have feelings. Conflicts are inescapable. Making it violent is the wrong thing. Expressing displeasures through peaceful resolution of conflicts is right. It will make you understand each other better. "

I believe Laura's mum is right. Teach your child the importance of understanding the difference between peaceful resolution of a conflict versus their desires to end them in another, unfavourable solution. As Laura's mum espouses, it's good to let the teen know how to overcome conflicts. They should understand that trials and crisis are part of life, and should not resort to hatred or malice, nor should run away from people in conflict with. Conflicts build spines and develop one's personality for the real world.

54. Teach your child that he/she cannot make a wish to make a conflict disappear; they have to deal with it.

Conflict will not resolve on its own. Disagreements are meant to be solved by talking and apologising as necessary. A conflict does not disappear or resolve itself by making a wish. Laura's mum also added that discarding her feeling as if it doesn't matter and wishing the problem disappears won't happen. If Laura pretends as if she isn't hurt and her feelings don't matter, Lillian might go ahead and do another worse thing that would hurt her. As she listened to her mum, Laura sighed and let the words sink in.

55. Teach your teen to tackle the problem and not the person.

Conflict happens as a result of a particular issue, but because of a specific person. Teach your teen not to make disagreements personal.. e next day, Laura told Lillian she wanted to see her shortly after prep. They did meet and here is their conversation:

Laura: Why did you do that?

Lillian: Do what?

Laura: Why did you send that message?

Lillian: Nothing. It was fun.

Laura: Did you know I was hurt?

Lillian: You were? But you told me nothing about it after that day. I had no idea. I am truly sorry.

Laura: Please, I don't want you to do that again. It is not fun to me and every guy in school thinks I am a cheap girl.

Lillian: Oh no! I am sorry, Laura. But we were all just playing. Anyway, I will go tell them I was the one that did it.

Laura: Oh no! Don't do that. The whole thing has died down already. There is no reason to awaken a sleeping tiger.

Lillian: Are you sure about that?

Laura: Yes I am. Look Lillian, I just told you so that you would know I did not appreciate what you did. I should have said it previously but I felt it could result in conflict and I don't want that. Anyway, I have stated my mind now.

Lillian: I am so sorry, Laura. I won't hurt your feelings again.

Laura: [silence]

Lillian: Laura, say something.

Laura: Best friends?

Lillian: Best friends [they hug].

And that's it. You can't wish the problem didn't happen. It did. The person involved is just an agent. The real deal is the problem. Even if the scenario does not resolve itself as peacefully as the one above, it is crucial for your child to understand the necessity of telling others how they feel about conflicts in the future.

One of my grandmother's most important pieces of advice was to let things go as quickly as they come, always to remember that when there is a problem, only you can provide a meaningful solution. A heart that has achieved peace would not be perturbed by anything of little or no meaning. If you would not remember it in a couple of days, weeks, if it won't matter in a couple of months, you should not spend a second being bothered about it.

56. Teach your teen to be respectful.

Be calm and listen to the other person. Looking at that time may come as a drag, but running away will not solve the issue either. Listen to the other person. Listening is an essential part of conflict resolution.

57. Consider being assertive, not aggressive or passive.

Dealing with teen conflicts doesn't require the teen to be aggressive or passive. By being assertive, teens should put their views forward calmly and confidently. Being aggressive or passive distracts from the conflict at hand.

58. Teach your teen to negotiate.

Negotiation is a necessary skill that every teenager is expected to learn. This skill goes beyond the present; it's a skill that will serve in the long term. Until your teen learns and knows how to compromise with others, they will find it difficult to resolve conflicts. Teach your teen that he/she can't win all disputes. At times, the best way to solve conflict is to let the other person win; that is, give the other person what he wants. These experiences will also come with time.

Now, your teen may feel that giving room for the other person to win isn't fair. This is the best time to encourage your teen that life isn't always balanced. You can reduce the blow of this harsh life lesson by explaining that there are times when one loses, and there are times one wins. Introduce the idea of negotiation, where both sides give a little for the sake of conflict resolution.

59. Stick to the present.

During conflict resolution, do not refer to past issues; doing that will only worsen the conflict. Often, teenagers have constant conflicts with the same person, say, a best friend or sibling. Having disputes with the same person will bring up negative experiences with the person. Chances are, when a conflict happens again with the same person, there will be a higher level of resentment towards the person, and this makes it difficult to resolve the current dispute.

So, encourage your teen to forget about the past negative experiences with the said person. Let your teen know that there's nothing that can be done to change what had happened in the past. Instead of linking the negative experience of the past to the present, they should let go of the past and focus on resolving the conflict at hand to better their future.

60. Silent treatment will not work.

Being silent or withdrawn is as bad as being aggressive. This won't solve the problem. Just talk it out with the person in conflict.

61. Teach your teen to be understanding, not defensive.

Analyse the situation and try putting yourself in the other person's shoe. Listen to the other person to understand their point of view. Don't build walls to defend yourself.

62. Teach your teen to say sorry.

Let your teen stand in front of the mirror and practice to say sorry. Teach your teen that saying sorry doesn't make one weak, but secure. Saying sorry even when one has done nothing wrong doesn't make one soft, but stronger. I am not disputing that it might sound complicated for a teen to say sorry, especially when he/she is not wrong; but it is an attitude, not an act; and the earlier your teen learns this attitude, the better for him/her.

63. Encourage your child to talk about the conflict.

If you find that your teen has a conflict with a peer or friend, encourage him/her to sit with the concerned person and talk it out. Let her know that it's okay to express her feelings to the other person, and to listen to the other person too. In fact, listening to the other person and their problems can often lead to the problem getting solved The other person might not want to talk about the conflict, but the person that proceeds toward resolving conflict is the mature one. Encourage your child to be knowledgeable about conflict. Let the two parties talk about it. At the end of the day, they will both discover that the battle was just a misunderstanding, a minor one at that.

64. Give your teen space to settle the conflict on

his/her own; but assure them you'll be there to help if needed.

Learning to resolve issues and conflicts on their own will help your teen blossom into a better person with strong communication skills.

These commandments are conflict resolution skills that will not only help teens deal with conflicts, but also solve life issues they will face throughout life in general. You need to understand that not every teen will readily follow these commandments; so you need to try over and over again. Most teenagers just want to do things their way at first, but over time they may begin to see the benefits of doing things for others.

They believe they are in charge and their parents should be their backup plan. I know you don't like the sound of it, but that is the truth. As a parent, you cannot lose patience. Take a deep breath and recall that you were once a teenager. It's critical to start early enough before they turn into rebels. You have to be there for them.

What is true is that when the teen has a conflict with society, they for the most part submit and agree with the status quo or agree with the situation in the present as things stand. They might not agree with it, but their conviction is not strong enough to confront the situation. But a person that has spine takes a stand and changes the belief of others; that is what Martin Luther was saying that to lose his value was to lose himself. He meant, there has to be something that you are so convinced about as to give your life for it, values you will rather die for than to compromise.

As for children between the ages of 3 and 8, grafting values in them and establishing them in these truths will help them fight for it such that no storm will take them from it. A child adequately groomed in these truths does not allow the tide of the circumstance of life to change him or her.

"One of the biggest challenges when raising strong-willed kids is that they don't listen and parents give up. You want to be very selective about the things you are going to discipline for or else you will end up in constant power struggles with your child" [13]. So, while it's essential to prepare your child for any 'storm', it's necessary to find a balance that doesn't result in a power struggle.

Usually, children of this age group are guided by their feeling, emotion and self-interest. They are driven by immediate gratification, and don't have the ability to see or look far into the future. They are ready to cross any border; only what they see now matters.

Helen thought it was impossible not to do what others are doing. She suffered, but she decided to live by the invisible values she had learned. Yes, she ached to keep these values. She suffered as a student, not having what most of her friends have, things like modern phones which her parents could not afford. She persevered with her invisible values. She was focused, hardworking, had integrity; she was a faithful friend, diligent at her studies, and well-disciplined, qualities that made her more productive than others of her colleagues years later.

These values were not visible then, but one day all these invisible values gave her what others could not get. She did not follow those friends who were disobeying the law to acquire things. But years later, she could afford most of the things her friend could not afford.

Material things are temporal; she says to herself. A car can break down. So it makes no sense to base one's life on such things. You might not even lose them, but you are not rich because you have a car.

The real values are like a guiding light that leads a child's way through life. People who have values, regard it above their life. People without values lack moral spine or standards of living to hold them firm through life's upheavals; so wherever the wind blows is where the tide takes them.

It's much better to guide your child towards developing well-rounded views and personality traits than to have them focus on the instant gratification of using social media on their brand new smartphone. Guide them towards appreciating the small things and learning something new every day.

6

COMMUNICATION SKILLS

Communication skills are essential for teens. Employers, teachers and college admissions staff expect teens to communicate well and effectively. This section talks about the strategies parents can adopt to help their teens develop communication skills.

Good enough, kids like to talk, and could be very loquacious when at their level. So, stop being the commander with kids; such overbearing posture could make them withdraw and afraid to talk. Be their friend and build the bridge of communication. Don't be authoritarian. Talk their language. Share with them your own experience at their age. Remember:

1. Your children carry your DNA. This, however, does not mean they will follow you in what you do or that they are copying your practices.

2. Children must be raised intentionally. So, assemble the child by laws and principles. Design a rigid schedule for each day to form and create meaningful impact into your children, with values you would like to see in them at least. Design a 20-30-minute period each day or minimum twice

a week for teaching your child the values you'd like to see in them. You could have a topic for a whole week: e. g. pick an article on Feeling and Emotions, read through it together, ask questions and analyse it.

3. Raising children is about giving instructions, not by emotions or feelings. Build character and core values in the child to provide them with moral.

4. Construct a concrete definitive value system to permit the child to abide by the values you have set, and to help the child find a purpose for living. Parenting is to help connect purpose and to live a goal- and purpose-driven life. To give the child a purpose, parenting must have an agenda that give the child a sense of mission.

I remember once speaking to a parent who wondered why she was not getting on with her child. She would use terms like "I let her do what she wants" and "She's just like me, we're too alike". Both of these statements can be problematic when it comes to effective communication. As stated above, children should be in a routine, developing their organisational skills. Your child needs to also be themselves, with their own identity. It only makes things worse when you refer to them as being 'too much like you'.

65. Create time to talk to your child.

Do not let going to school, engaging in sports and carrying out other activities by your child debar you from a moment with him/her. You need to make time to talk to your child. And when your teen starts driving, you shouldn't be chatting with him/her as you used to when you drove. It's essential to have conversations with your teen in a very relaxed atmosphere. Spend time with them when they need you. Don't trade children's time for other activities.

Anything you want can only be bought with time. The currency we all have is time, whatever you give time, you get in return. To gain the respect of a child you have to buy time by providing time, investing your time to that child; that way you learn to respect the child. Go out with them intentionally to be able to enjoy their company. Don't let it surprise you, children look forward to time alone with their parents. Make time for them as you would the rest of your family and friends. Even if they decide they don't want to spend time with you, they appreciate that you've tried.

By creating time for your children, you build values in them. Your son does not appreciate it when you're not there. Your continual and perpetual absence could hurt your children for the rest of their life, and they would judge you for it. Don't elevate your work or duties above your children. Don't say I am making money for you. That's not what they want, they want you to spend time with them, not just to provide shelter, clothes and food. To children, your presence means love.

"The concern over the scarcity of family time is linked to growing scholarly interest in how adolescents spend their time. Conceptualised as socialisation contexts, the allocation of time to different activities has important implications for adolescent development" [14].

Also, children don't want you manipulating them to get them to do things; they don't want to detect lies in your dealings with them; they want to be sure you are real. Did you promise to do something? Then deliver. If you lie to them, your children will accuse and tell you to your face you don't deserve their respect.

In your talk with your children, they want to hear more compliment and supportive words; so do less and less of judgmental speaking. Acknowledge your children more. If you neglect to talk with them, you ruin the relationship. Mind you, being physically absent is the same as there but absent-minded. When you don't hear them, all because you are cooking or about something else, it's all the same as you were not there. Your absent-mindedness means you are not in their life or they are not in yours. So, try to be consciously involved, not abstractly involved. Repeat to your children what has been said to affirm to them that you are listening. When you don't respond it communicates neglect to them.

Don't do or dream of other things that might make your children feel unloved and neglected. Be present and let the child know you are listening and can hear them with every fibre of your body. Some daughters feel ignored, and not worth talking to when parents fail to hold a typical conversation with them. This is why when you now want them to hear you they don't listen because you did not listen to them. The same reaction will ensue if you were always lost when they are talking to you. They pay back by not responding to you.

"Relationships between parents and their children are greatly improved when there is effective communication taking place. In general, if communication between parents and their children is good, then their relationships are good as well" [15].

Talking to your teen helps them to practice ahead for interactions with other people outside the family. Choose a regular time, one that works for you and your teen, to talk. You can schedule family dinners with no TV, or weekly walk-and-talk to communicate with your teen.

For instance, Rooney was arrested at a club with some other guys who are his friends as suspects of hard drugs transporters. . ney's mum rushed to the police station the second day to bail out her son after the other guys justified him.

But his mum got so worried and asked him why he had to go to the club in the first place until he was keeping the company of drug dealers. You know what Rooney said?

"I don't even know why we are having this conversation in the first place. If you'd been talking to me like this for years, my life would have been better. I know dad's dead but I expect you always to talk and communicate with me. I felt so lonely. You know those guys are my best of friends even though I don't deal in drugs as they did. I wished I was still in jail with them. It is much more interesting there with them. Now, I have to keep on with my lonely life again. "

This scenario proves how important it is to create the needed bond with your child from a young age. Sadly, Rooney then walked out and his mum fainted but was rushed to the hospital.

I know this story sounds emotional; but you don't know the next teen on the line. So, protect your teen by talking to them always. Allow children to make different mistakes so that they can learn the appropriate lessons. Yes, we don't want our children to make mistakes, and that's why we control them. But again, they're only human and it's inevitable that it will happen at some point. It's just important how you manage and control those situations.

Yes, by their tendency, children, especially teenagers, don't like to ask for help; they want you to trust them. Yet, they need you most, even though they push you away. They know what to say to make you feel bad so you don't come to them and make you leave them alone. They don't express themselves to say they need help or they are vulnerable. But they are. Talking about things opens the way for a closer relationship, and makes bonding easier and better. "Trust is an abstract concept, and concrete examples can give your teen a better understanding of how to be trustworthy" [16].

Admitting your fault is honourable. A lot of folks have made grievous mistakes concerning child upbringing. As you can imagine, child upbringing is not about what to wear or what to eat and making sure your child is not worse than his colleagues at school and kids in the neighbourhood. Sending your child to a right school, making sure the child is well dressed, clean, well-fed and looking pretty; good as they are, all of those are not all that is needed. There is much more to being a good parent.

Raising children is with a purpose to form in him a personality. You have to help the child discover their personality before they leave home. One parent once told me about their child and he couldn't pinpoint exactly who he was, using the phrase "I don't know who I am". That parent then had the job of not only guiding their child to discovering who he was but also calming his nerves and reassuring him that everything he was feeling was natural and perfectly normal.

Many children can get older and older without actually discovering who they really are or what their personality is. We are not just to be concerned about what we see physically about the child but the personality of the child. A child is not only the body. Outside, they speak good English and dress well, but their character is not formed, the person within is not discovered yet. You need to guide the child to find out who they are.

A child might not drink or smoke, but might not have developed a proper personality. We must have a system and a goal in place, not just saying: smoking is wrong or, don't have a sexual relationship, or threatening to discipline the child if found in any such disgusting behaviour. A proper personality is also not just about greeting people well, and visitors saying your child is well raised or has good manners. Those proper conducts may well be occasional or programmed for the right occasion.

To form the proper personality in your child, raise the child in a programme or schedule, a routine to guide the child intentionally to discover the personality you aim. Each day, aim to do something with the child. It may not be more than 30 minutes every day, but choose a topic to teach to achieve the core values of the personality they should become. Take them through the periods of value formation. "Many studies on personality distinguish three types: resilience, over controllers, and under controllers. This typology is based on the theory of ego-control and ego-resiliency by Block and Block" [17].

Whether your child is a 'resilient' or an 'under controller', help them to understand who they are, take pride in it and flourish. It will do them a world of good when it comes to their overall attitude, positivity and determination, giving them every chance to accept who they are and go on to succeed.

From ages 5-12, you may want to spend say, an hour drilling into their minds systematic instructions, so that by age 14 they know where they are; e. g. how not to fall under pressure, how to overcome trials and conflicts. . . . This is systematic parenting and nurturing. If you don't have a systematic way of training your child, what will happen is that the baby will be fed, have fun, go to school, do all those expected things, but nothing is constructed within. The child is just growing in the body, the inside is not increasing. The consequence of that is that no anchor is provided to hold and secure the child in times of emotional crises. The child is empty in the core; he is not anchored, and lacks any direction in life and would not know what to do at the right time.

A child with just a body and a name is like windblown away. He is empty because he does not have an internal structure or spine to hold him up in the time of crises. He is like a ship without a compass, nothing to navigate him from inside. Such a child will be living only for himself, without a direction for proper neighbourliness with others in society. Children must have the inner mechanism for stability in life; else, they might stumble and fall. But they will be able to stand because of the internal balance of their value-based personality.

If a child has values, he will rule over his emotion; he sees himself as having his life as a means to accomplish the purpose for which he was created. Life is about purpose. A kid's life and personality are to be equipped for purposeful living. Life must be intentional for a goal. A kid's purpose and intent in life must be stocked for them from when they are small. "Children thrive when they have secure, positive relationships with adults who are knowledgeable about how to support their development and learning" [18]. Do everything you can to show them the way for purposeful living. They will grow up to thank you, and in later life, likely use the same techniques you used on them but with their own children.

66. Tackle touchy topics.

Encourage your teen to chat with you about touchy topics. They may pick up such issues from a newspaper, news events broadcast on radio and TV. They can also find subjects on social media or a discussion that started in a classroom. When your teen talks to you about current happenings and events, especially the complex ones, they find it easy to sort their thoughts on a particular subject and voice their opinion.

Some parents lay rules for the kind of topics to be discussed. This will not be helpful. Your teenager should be free to discuss any issue with you, including emotional and sexual feelings. That way, it makes it easier to advise them. Here is an example:

Father: What is it son? You are looking like you have seen a ghost.

Son: I don't know dad. There is this new girl in school and she is really...you know?

Father: Pretty?

Son: Yeah and so much attractive. I think I've got feelings for her.

Father: What feelings son?

Son: I don't know dad. I just like her.

Father: Son what you are going through is absolutely normal; in fact, I will be astonished if you don't have that as a human being. You can't see a beautiful flower and pretend it is not pleasant.

Son: Uh! I thought you would be mad at me for having thoughts like that instead of studying.

Father: No, I am not mad at you; but there are questions to ask around it.

Son: What questions?

Father: Are you ready to get married soon?

Son: No dad. That's not important right now.

Father: So what is essential; that you really like that girl because she is beautiful and probably curvy and you are thinking of sleeping with her?

Son: Dad? I...

Father: Look, son, I know about these things; and trust me, I know how your body feels. Before I permit you, I want to ask you some things.

Son: Okay dad.

Father: On a scale of 0 to 10, I want you to rate how much you know about this girl we are talking about?

Son: Hmmm, well, not so well, so I say 3.

Father: Okay son. Are you ready to leave school and get a job?

Son: No dad.

Father: Are you ready to get responsible for any pregnancy or father a child?

Son: Not yet dad.

Father: So you see. Considering what you said, you barely know this girl; plus, you are not ready to own up a pregnancy or father a child. So why not put your body under control and wait till you are much mature and responsible. I know your body wants it now but you ask yourself, am I ready for this? What if something happens after that, will I be able to own up? Would you have loved it if you were an outcome of a meaningless affair I had with just any woman when I was not very ready or responsible for it?

Son: No dad, I won't be happy.

Father: So, that is it, son. Why bring what doesn't matter into the picture now? I tell you, these things can be controlled. But you have to manage it yourself and not be hasty. Am I right?

Son: Yes dad.

Father: Having a relationship now will drain your strength. You can use those thoughts to gain content, and when you have content as a man, you will have choice of girls. So, what do you say, son?

Son: I will wait till when I am much mature and responsible.

Father:You must know that there is a great attraction between opposite sexes; that is natural after we are 12 or 13 years old, especially now with TV and the Internet. For some kids, even from as early as nine years old is when the attraction of the opposite sex starts. And you cannot fulfil it for another 10- 15 years. That is until you are disciplined enough and prepared to get married. So, you have got to master that feeling you have. You are not to kill it outright; just master it. It is when you deny it of strength that your personality strength becomes stronger. But if you give in to every desire of yours, you become a slave of that desire. If you are too close with someone of the opposite sex, it is like holding two polarised magnets together. How far can you hold two magnets together without it touching. They will always contact when you bring them close. If they are far away you can keep them apart; but the closer you bring them together the greater and stronger their attraction. Just as magnets pull together without you hunting it, so it is when a boy and a girl come close, even when they determine not to touch each other.

Son: Ok dad.

Father: Thank you, son.

You know what? Until you reach a stage like this in the conversation between you and your teen, you are still trying. It may sound impossible for a twenty-first-century parent and child, but here is the good news, it is possible. It all depends on lowering your ego as a parent, coming to the level and understanding of the feelings of your teen. This understanding is a big thing for teens. Some of their opinions would be wrong, but respect them nonetheless.

If you take the words of your teachers seriously, your life will reflect it. Similarly, the words of parents formulate or reflect who children become. If your father had told you about diligence and you took it seriously, you very likely evolved a diligent personality. You become what your attitude is to words. So, don't trivialise the words you say to your children as a parent. Words produce the quality of who your children will become. You're having a much more significant impact on your child than you could ever even imagine. Attempt not to push your agenda but the importance of developing their own individual thought processes and living practices. Every word you say counts, and may be used by them later on.

Most children don't open up. So you must ask them questions for them to open up. If you don't support them by asking them questions they will be enticed with their friends' answers, which could be wrong anyway, with the dire consequence that can have on their life. Yet, that sorry end you can avoid just by paying attention to their peculiarities, especially for kids between ages 8 and 11 years. Parents should know that children will have behaviour changes, not always in the direction they desire; so be ready for that. Such changes could make them assume a dominant posture. They want to embrace their own opinions, not yours. One parent told me how their child was repeating things she had said at home. She had only found this out because she had found her daughter's social media profile and saw posts relating to what her mum had said. The child was not embracing who she was, but mimicking her mother's behaviour, views and attitudes. It's essential to avoid creating this situation and allow them to develop and then embrace their own opinions.

It is the hormones that make them act that way. So, expect new behaviours that you were not seeing before, new tendencies you were not seeing previously, like sexual interest, and the desire to hang out with friends. You have to manage new situations. One suggestion is that you look for music that is funny, live their life, take an interest in scary things. Except you are prepared for these sort of changes, you could be worried. We are to use our thinking faculty to overrule our instinct faculty when dealing with teenagers.

67. Enforce good listening skills.

It's essential that you teach your teen to pay attention when someone is conversing with them. Guidance counsellors and teachers want to be listened to and understood when they speak. Teach your teen to ask questions politely when he/she doesn't hear or comprehend someone. To demonstrate this, pay full attention when your child is having a conversation with you. Some 75% of broken relationships are as a result of one person not listening to the other. So, don't just teach listening skills, demonstrate it also. Capacity to listen will help and reduce the likelihood of a broken relationship.

68. Teach your child how to find common ground for conversation.

As a young adult, having a conversation with an adult may be daunting if the young adult lacks communication skills. Finding common ground with a speaker or a peer requires practice. Whenever your child shares a story or an incident with you, ask your child to repeat some of what was said; or you do so yourself, to demonstrate you were listening and that you care. Ask him/her questions. Then go on to talk about your day, and encourage your teen to ask you questions also.

Your teen might ask you really weird or strange questions. It is not for you to start suspecting them. They want to trust you. By making your teen ask you questions, you enable them to develop trust in you.

Over time, communication will become natural, not forced, and you and your teen will reap the benefits of increased communication skills.

69. Encourage your teen to take advantage of social media platforms.

Does your child use social media platforms such as Instagram, Facebook or Twitter? The photos and tweets shared by the users your child follows can fuel conversation the next time they meet. On the flip side, if your son/daughter doesn't know how to start conversations, her activities on social media will make it a bit easier for her followers and friends to walk up to her in person and start a discussion. However, understand that social media platforms have their downsides, with their adverse effects. So, your child may need extra support if complications should arise on that front. In the digital world of today, social media is a breeding ground for negativity, bullying and harassment. Where teenagers can make a post at the tap of a smartphone touch screen, it's more important than ever before for both parents and teenagers to be well versed in the ins and outs of social media, it's benefits, it's drawbacks and the effect it can have on the child's social life and personality.

Helen is a mother of three teenagers, namely: Sean is 14, Mikey 12, and Deb is 10. Helen goes to see her friend, Sheila, who is like an aunt to her, to discuss the effect of social media on her children. Sheila has more grown-up children who have been well brought up, and Helen really loves what she sees when she goes to Sheila for a cup of tea, and would like her children to be more like Sheila's children. Here is their conversation:

Helen: Children these days are deeply affected by social media; it's like a modern-day legal high in so many ways, it's actually terrifying, but people of all ages love it. The kids are growing up in an era different from how I have grown up. I did not grow up addicted to social media.

Sheila: So true. I did not grow up addicted to it as well. But we must all accept this new reality and deal with it.

Helen; I have just observed that Mikey, my 12-year-old boy is addicted to being on his phone, it's a daily occurrence at this point. You know when you see him, it won't be long before his face is buried in his smartphone. He sees the people he's speaking to on there almost every day in person, yet he's still being devoured by this addiction to social media. It's almost like it's more appealing to communicate over technology because you don't get the same thoughts and feelings from it. It's different, nerves and any anxiety you have go out of the window, but being on there opens you up to vulnerability and pain, I don't know if he really knows that yet.

Sheila: As a teacher, I try to negotiate with students so that it is not a cause for conflict. But it becomes a portal for a deeper connection. Children are growing up on a diet of social media, and this is an intricate part of their life and our life too. This is what is feeding the soul of our young ones. We all have to accept it as a new thing.

Helen: I have come to accept the fact that social media has come to stay; it is here, and it is now. I have tried to stop Mikey's Instagram and snap chat, but no result. Children will find a way to use it and hide it away from us. So I have decided that there is no point fighting it at all, because it will be a pointless battle or conflict all the time on the same issue. The best we can do is encourage them of the benefits of not relying on it for all communication. But, what can we do? It's all around them; it's their tablets, their smartphones, their smartwatches, their games consoles. Social media is everywhere.

Sheila: You are right. The social media have come to stay. The next thing to enforce is limits and boundaries; those are the way we feel safe. Our children need limits and boundaries, but not created at the spur of the moment, but as needs to be lived and embodied.

Helen: That will mean as a parent, I must have boundaries first in my own life so that I am not hypocritical. Last Tuesday, I was working on my phone using Facebook to post a comment to my boss and Mikey sees me, and queries why I stopped his Instagram when I could freely use Facebook. It was challenging to explain to him that when I go on Facebook, it is for my work but Instagram is for pleasure, which I was not after at the moment. He found it hypocritical to say that Facebook is for my work when I use it, and when he does use Instagram, it was for pleasure. "This is hypocrisy," he said to me. It's almost like he's not willing to listen to rational thinking, because he thinks he needs to defend his tendencies to rely on social media. He's addicted but doesn't want it pointing out. I imagine most children are this way now.

Sheila: You could have shown him what you were doing. As parents, we must not practice double standards. Children must not feel we are imposing on them something we do not wish to impose on our self. That will not be healthy. We need to show we are supporting them while giving them the freedom to evaluate their own choices and come to their conclusions, sometimes.

Helen: Well, I did not show him the details. I only expected him to know that I was working.

Sheila: As parents, we have to be present and involved in our children's life. When we eat dinner at the table or when on the train, we cannot be glued to our phone screen, and on social media, fail to create a healthy boundary with the social media, and expect our children to change their habits with the social media. Breaking habits is going to be much harder than anybody could ever imagine.

Helen: Ok, so you're saying this is what Mikey is seeing. But how can I get him to leave his social media, which is so seductive?

Sheila: What of Sean, your first?

Helen: He has gotten so addicted to it.

Sheila: How about Deb, your daughter?

Helen: She finds it so entertaining and enticing as well.

Sheila: You have got your solution in your hands, friend!

Helen: How?

Sheila: You will have to create a better relationship with your kids, better than what you have now. Your relationship with the three of them lacks the things you mentioned; that's the reason they are looking for it in social media.

Helen: How?

Sheila: You will have to be more exciting, more entertaining; which you do well for your friends but not for your kids. Be meaningful, real for and with the children. Being authentic is the best you can do, real is relatable and it's probably how you get the best results.

Helen: So true!

Sheila: Why will the children leave what makes them happy and come to you, even though you do much for them and work so hard. They simply are not getting what they want, so they go to where they can get it and satisfy their desire, which is also never met. I'll come round your house on Saturday to visit, since you are all in and see your typical Saturday.

On the appointed day.

Sheila: I have seen that they come to you and all you do to them is ridicule MIKEY, shame SEAN, and control DEB. So they go to hide in social media. It's an escape from the harsh realities of life. Almost like they can't deal with things if they can't turn to their digital devices. You must make the relationship with your Mikey more joyful, then with SEAN more connecting, so that they are more drawn to YOU rather than hiding in social media away from you.

Helen: How?

Sheila: Don't look at social media as a threat. Embrace it while informing of the drawbacks of excessive use. It's a very complex beast, so don't fight it - but find a way that makes it work.

Helen: Oh, there is a positive aspect which I know but not applied. There is a vibrant way to use social media that is healthy, not in a way that is co-dependent, so when I post something and I do it because I am enmeshed and addicted to how many likes I get and glued to my phone screen, I was a bad example to the kids.

Sheila: They watch you so closely. They have seen it all. If you use social media to elevate a sense of SELF, you will be modelling that for the children who will in turn model social media for a sense of worth. But if you use social media as an avenue and a portal for connection with the world, then you will teach your children that technology is a vibrant technology. That to me is a fertile foundation.

Parents/carers must be aware of how they model their relationship with social media. It is through your modelling that your children will absorb how to use it in a positive way rather than in a co-dependent and addictive way.

70. Roleplay conversation with your child.

A teen who looks forward to social interactions is confident to walk into them. Whether your child is going to the prom or a college fair, help him/her practice what to say to other people during the event. Show your teen how to adjust to the tone and conversation topics that work for both adults and other teens. Roleplay conversation by taking the role of each person expected to be at the prom so your child can have first-hand knowledge of the scenarios to expect at the event, and can be better prepared for those situations.

71. Clarify body language.

Kids that have trouble communicating may find it challenging to pick up on nonverbal cues, otherwise known as body language. In some scenarios, these kids may not even be aware of their own body language. There's a lot you can take from somebody's body language, especially your child's body language. Ranging from a blank face to a transfixed state, there are several interpretations you can take from these physical cues [19].

The truth is, body language significantly affects how your child is seen in interviews for programmes, jobs or college. A day before the meeting, use a video camera or a Smartphone with a video app to record your child answering practice questions to help prepare them for their interview. After that, watch the footage and come up with ideas for improvements as required.

For instance, your teen has a crucial scholarship interview in the next few weeks. Cr. e time for her to practice. Be the judge and sit in front of an office table. Let her practice her walking steps, body gestures, sitting postures, eye contacts, confidence and all of that. As long as the practice continues, she will catch up and become confident. This practice will prove most beneficial in the long run to help your teen open doors of opportunities.

You have to get ready for the opportunity, to grasp the moment and opportunity and catch it even when things fail daily. Different occasions will come when you don't expect. Opportunities come to people who are always improving themselves. The illustration of the ant that provides its food in summer, and gathers it in during harvest is very striking. Working in summer is like preparing or developing yourself awaiting winter or the moments of opportunities that will come your way.

Life demands more than what we all are comfortable with. Not preparing for opportunities that will come is the reason why a lot of people are going through hard times not knowing what to do. We have to get our teen/young adult to step out of their comfort zone, get a holiday job and learn the skills they need for better openings in the future. They must undergo the pain of discipline or they feel the pain of disappointment. "Improving children's resilience helps them to deal with the adversities they experience during childhood. It provides a foundation for developing skills and habits (e. g. coping skills, healthy thinking habits) that enable them to deal with later adversities during adolescence and adulthood" [20]. Building resilience in your child teaches them the discipline needed in order to not only survive, but thrive - taking on each challenge they're faced with in early life and their adult years.

When kids discover who they are, they see that no one is better than them. No one is better than them in doing what they have to do. Self-development helps kids discover their potential. We can help kids to know that other people are not better than them, so they don't give an excuse. People might have natural talent which they might not have, but each child can also discover their talent which others don't have. We all can help our children tap into the treasure in them. It is not by the connections they don't have, but by the opportunities that will come their way. So, we are to encourage study, research and get the best out of them; to go into themselves, cultivate their gift, and do their best in their specific area.

As mentioned earlier, the key focus is to hone in on oneself, rather than comparing to others. This isn't just important to push with our children but is something that should follow one through life. Particularly in the digital age of today where people are gaining popularity and fame from their talents, giving them much greater exposure than they would have got twenty years ago, it's easy to get yourself out there now. Well, that's provided that the talent has been developed.

Rather than focusing on a child's concern or worries over a lack of talent, it's essential to offer quality time together and assist them in 'putting it right', if you believe it would help them then you should attempt to partake in activities to 'discover' your child's true potential.

People who are succeeding brought out the best in themselves and the world or environment around applauded them. Zoe, a year eight girl decided to cultivate herself and use her situation and environment to bring the best out of her. She made the best of what she was given and stopped complaining. She fought her limitation, she kept them. She stopped fighting, knowing that geniuses are made, not born she thought. If you don't work hard though you still will not be your best she told herself. Anyone can be great; it depends on the effort you put into what you do, she told herself so she added motivation, persistence and determination, then she had an outstanding GCSE result in her year 11.

Life is not as easy as the school system. Kitty, who is friends with Zoe was average at school and Zoe told her that School does not define great geniuses. Even if you do poorly in school you can still develop yourself. Academic power is not synonymous to wealth. You can get straight A's, yet live an empty life if you miss vital opportunities.

72. Play word games.

There are quite a number of classic games that teach language skills to kids with learning or communication issues. While playing the game, your child may be oblivious of the interaction going on with others due because the game is exciting and fun. Recall Tip 2 earlier on Emotional Charades. Ask players to act different scenes while other kids guess what they are acting. These games help kids concentrate on the body language of people among them.

73. Be critics together.

More than often, employers, friends and college admissions staff ask your teens the books they are reading, movies they are watching, or other interests they might have. So, choose a book, be it ebook or paperback, to read together. You can even watch a live performance or a movie together. Afterwards, talk about the highlights of the book or the film, and how they might respond to answers to those questions in an interview if issues were to arise. Ask your child what she liked and disliked about the characters, or the plot of the book. Was there a part or scene that she doesn't understand?

Asking and answering this sort of questions keep your child engaged in the story which is an essential skill that will be useful to your child when conversing with others. Fix a time every day to meet together and address subjects of mutual importance, say, Responsibility. Read a chapter on the subject and dialogue on it. Building and drilling down values in a fun way by putting them in intentionally will affirm them, not just saying, "I told you not to do it?" or "Why did you do it?" Such emotional outbursts can't be enough.

We all have to develop the mind of our kids. Make them think critically. Answer their questions so to improve their memory. Remember, they may be asking 'silly questions' but they're only silly because the answer is evident in your fully-developed brain. Make your kids develop focus and concentration from as early as Age 7. Develop their ability to study, speak and memorise, all involving a thinking faculty. These will help the child view himself right, and see himself as a person to be respected. While the development process proceeds, don't compare your child to other children, as this could create an inferiority complex. Witness what they are able to achieve and embrace it, embrace your child.

Help them to be fluent and vocal by asking them questions and allowing them to defend their opinions. Give them topics and addresses to speak on and talk about. Give your child assignments to stir up their ability to speak their mind and defend their points, assignments that develop their ability to present their ideas before people and not be intimidated, and fully express what was learnt at school. Get the child to work and love the work that they are putting into developing themselves and their views. "Listening to young children can create the time and space in which they can reflect on their early year's experience and in so doing, help them to process and understand what is happening. 'It's not so much a matter of eliciting children's preformed ideas and opinions, it's much more a question of enabling them to explore how they perceive the world and communicate their ideas in a way that is meaningful to them" [21].

Understand that from as early as the age of three, children are already able to think creatively [22]. That's why they could break things and put them together; they could experiment, look at things that interest them. So, look out for the child's special interest areas. Traits of complex fields as engineers can be seen in a child from as early as Ages 3 to 7. Give as much scope of life as possible to enable the child to discover the world.

74. Encourage your teen to consider blogging or journaling.

Keeping a journal or a diary helps your child to express his/her feelings and thoughts. When children write about their daily activities, they can think through what had happened in the day, and become more confident and prepared to talk to others about those events. The thought process or thinking ability of a child can be developed. There are laws guiding the process.

- 1st Law of Thought: You must be purposeful, targeting an answer to a specific question.
- 2nd Law of Thought: All thoughts must attempt to answer a question.
- 3rd Law of Thought: All thoughts are based on assumptions.

Questioning is the foundation of understanding of anything in life. Anyone can go from an idiot to a genius just by asking the right questions. Once a child has asked the right questions: What should I do, what step should I take; their next step is what to do with the answers the child has got. Asking a question about the process they are interested in, and writing down the steps; then put them to work.

No child would empower himself/herself if they raised questions for questioning sake, except they want to task themselves to work with their answers. If children ask detail and purposeful questions, their answers should give them a goal to pursue. Their goals forms their vision; their vision creates passion that empowers their mission; and as we know, without a purpose their idea will be powerless, purposeless, lacking drive and no passion. The process therefore begins with questions, then answers, then vision and mission empowered by passion. A child who has been taught to ask the right questions will get the correct answers that produce vision, mission and purpose in life.

"Language is an instrument of human reason, and not merely a medium for the expression of thought, is a truth generally admitted" [23]. Developing something within your child from thought, to well-informed view to something they can express eloquently via language in the way they feel most comfortable with is something quite remarkable. If they're open to the idea of using blogging or journaling to voice these thought processes and develop their understanding of the world around them, you should encourage it.

7

MAKING YOUR KIDS HAPPY AND SUCCESSFUL

Every parent wants their children to be happy and successful. I do, and you do too. Yes, there are tons of parenting advice on the Internet; but the question is, who should we listen to? Whose answer is trustworthy? To provide answers to these questions, I have read dozens of research journals and scientific articles from which I have compiled a list. This section talks about the ways to bring up well-adjusted and confident children, and help them become the successful adults you have always wanted them to become. Home is the right environment for raising kids.

75. Become a happy parent yourself.

An emotionally disturbed parent will transfer the disturbing emotions to his/her kids. If a parent is emotionally disturbed, chances are their children will be disturbed emotionally. Unhappy parents have proved to be less effective parents. On the flip side, happy parents are capable parents, and are more likely to have happy kids. You'd be surprised that children wish that their parents are less tired and stressed out than they want them to spend time with them or give them freedom. Be a happy parent, and watch your kids grow up to become comfortable and better individuals.

76. Celebrate with your family, and as a family.

Happy families are the ones that celebrate big and small things. Whether this is a job promotion, festivals, holidays, and the end of a stressful week or a good grade, happy families always look for a reason to celebrate family achievements. You can keep the celebration simple by going to the park as a family or you can make the celebration elaborate by throwing a small party.

Happy families raise happy children; so endeavour to celebrate with your family often. Let your kids know what it means to celebrate and be satisfied – all the time. For instance, your kid won a debate that took him/her so much effort and time to prepare for. They are naturally happy and excited. You know what would make it much fun? Do your best to share in your child's happiness. You could get a bottle of chilled drink and just make a small party in your living room with the siblings joining in. You don't know how much entertaining it is and how much encouragement you are pumping into those kids when you treat their achievements like the celebrations they genuinely are.

77. Prioritise your marriage over your children.

Contrary to popular misconceptions, prioritising your marriage over your children helps to raise happy and successful kids. Why? Children want a settled home. Families that are centred on children will only create exhausted parents, anxious parents and demanding children. Today, parents are too quick to sacrifice their marriages and lives for their kids. As a parent, the greatest gift you can give your children is a settled home and a fulfilled marriage.

Here are some simple but useful clues that can help to strengthen your marriage:

- Complement each other through helping each other.
- Greet each other happily.

- Crave each other's company as best friends and companions.
- Eat together.
- Pray together.
- Go to church together.
- Be patient with each other.
- Listen to each other.
- Seek each other's opinion on every matter.
- Have no restricted property or resources against either partner.
- Be open with your phones and mobile devices, with no bounds on text messages, emails or other social media accounts.
- Share one bedroom.
- Proudly associate in all places, private or public, and when needed, joyfully introduce each other to the public.
- Show respect and honour in the way you address and talk to each other.
- Do all things always as a team, never as opponents or competitors.
- Even in games, compete passionately, but always playfully. Win some, but be sure to lose some too.
- Genuinely enjoy fun, share humour and laugh out loudly.
- Show genuine empathy and concern in each other's welfare.
- Be courteous to each other's parents and extended family.

Genuineness in all of these behaviours will easily be noticed and appreciated by your children, and will rest their hearts and mind about their settled home and the fulfilled marriage of their parents.

78. Give your children your engrossed attention when they talk to you.

Communicating with your kids is extremely important. If you want to raise happy children, then you need to communicate with them. Communicating properly with your kids doesn't just entail talking to them alone, it involves giving them undivided personal attention when they come to you with relevant news and activities of their day. Giving them your full attention means setting aside your electronic devices and newspapers, and listening attentively to them. When you communicate well and listen to your kids, your response will be thoughtful, and this will motivate your kids to be more communicative. Here is an odd example:

Daughter: Hey mum! I am talking to you. Can you leave your laptop for just a minute, please?

Mother: This is very important. I am listening Dora. I can't leave this laptop now. Just talk and say whatever it is you want to say. I am all ears.

Of course, this daughter is not going to be encouraged to tell her mum what she wants to say, and it could lead to a rapid loss of communication. If you know you are busy at that moment and you can't leave what you are doing, it is better to say something like:

"Look Dora, I know you want my attention right now but I really need to get on this stuff. Can you give me about an hour to finish this up so I could listen to you with full attention?"

Giving teens divided attention is like giving them the chance to be rebels. Full attention helps you to listen to unspoken words, like abuse or damaged reputation your kids have had with friends at school which might be challenging to express. You can offer a line of thought for the next action or decision. The truth is, nobody has time; but we all have to create the time for what must be done. This will help them feel more involved in family matters, and lead to better family communication. Many young people will choose to consult with their friends and peers over their parents.

You will find that your child will want to keep up with the latest trends, go to the busiest places and own the latest must-have gadget. In the UK, this will most likely be London, wearing expensive/higher-end high street brands and own the iPhone 11. Their friends and peers will most likely follow in this mindset too, and that's why nine times out of ten they will reason with their friends rather than you - it's a much simpler task. Parents will contrastingly push for more reasonably priced clothing, bought from the nearest shopping centre - and they'll say the iPhone 7 works just fine. As it does to me and you, but for a child it's so much different. These peers may have only appeared in their lives two weeks ago, but their opinion is worth so much more than yours in these development years.

As adults, we have seen and lived through our family proving over their entire lives that they are more valuable than our friends (there are exceptions of course). Generally they will feed you, dress you, put a roof over your head and spoil you with gifts and it's essential that your young ones realise the sacrifices you are making for them. Inform them of the sources of information they should trust and teach them that family is the most precious thing that should be closest to your heart.

79. Have regular meals together with your family.

Children who eat regular meals with their parents have been found to be more successful in every area, compared to those who don't. Such children get better grades in school, have high self-esteem and great self-confidence as well as an extensive vocabulary. Also, such children are less likely to smoke, take drugs, drink or develop psychological issues or addictions. Imagine your children getting all these rewards just by having frequent meals as a family.

When one person isn't around to eat with the family, probably he/she is on a journey; the whole family misses them and look forward to seeing him/her return to share the family mealtime again. Such togetherness gives the family a particular type of bond and unique harmony. A saying goes, "the family that eats together stays together. " This isn't just eating together as an event, or some form of ceremonial eating once a week and something to look forward to. It is about continuous, regular mealtime together as a family. It helps greatly.

80. Teach your kids to keep their emotions in check.

Kids who can manage their emotions tend to focus better, which is crucial for long term success. Such kids will even enjoy optimum physical and mental health. To help your kids keep their emotions in check, you should:

- Demonstrate emotional management yourself.
- Acknowledge the progress of your kids.
- Empathise with your kids and the emotions they are feeling.

81. Encourage your children to develop and keep meaningful relationships.

Having healthy and good relationships with peers and friends is crucial for the growth and psychological wellbeing of your children. Children who lack strong relationships do not do better in school, compared to those who do. Such children are likely to develop problems and could even get in trouble with the law. As a parent, an environment should be created deliberately that allows your children to build friendships. Teach them conflict resolution, and respond to their emotional cues. This makes children feel secure; and it forms the foundation for self-esteem.

Sleepover at a friend's place can help to cement lasting relationships for children. This is a time when your child goes to a sleepover with another family to learn and observe how things are mainly done differently in other homes, to observe similarities and differences. Sleepover helps practice social coping mechanism, and gives strength to relationships. It develops bonding with friends and can engender lifelong relationships which prove beneficial in the long run. Your children get to learn to invite friends home and treat them very well.

It is traumatic for young kids to be without friends. When young, children need the approval of parents; but as they grow older they seek the approval of peers. Many children don't know how to form deep and meaningful relationships. Many friendships are superficial, like Facebook likes. Social media relationships are hardly deep and meaningful. Except taught, children may not have the skillset, and may lack coping mechanisms to handle stress in relationships. This may explain why many children turn to social media relationships. This could become very frustrating for parents. When faced with challenges, such children tend to pour their emotions on social media contacts. Because such relationships have no strong foundations, your child could feel alone once those relationships begin to crumble.

There must be a balance to social media use. Sitting with friends and texting on a mobile device sends a message that you are not interested in the conversation; and the fact that you cannot put away your phone for the moment of the communication and interaction with friends shows you are addicted to social media and your phone. If at the least chance your child whips up his/her phone, the behaviour could destroy valuable relationships and opportunities that are happening around them.

It is worthy to maintain a good conversation with eye contact, and no phones interjecting, so you can form a good relationship. Talking and getting answers from the person you are talking to is ethical behaviour. These days, most kids cannot engage in meaningful conversation without an app or mobile device interjecting. This should be discouraged.

82. Set boundaries that are reasonable.

Parents who set and impose reasonable boundaries are the ones that raise successful and confident children. When you place a ground rule in the house, explain the principles behind the practice to your children. This helps to build a close relationship with your children. Do not over control, but set boundaries that will help your children reach their potentials. Firm disciplined boundaries help young ones know what they are allowed and what they are not.

83. Ensure that your children get enough sleep.

Studies have shown previously that children who do not get enough sleep:

- Find it difficult to focus.
- Have poor brain function.
- Lack creativity.
- Have high chances of becoming obese.
- Are usually unable to manage their emotions.

To help your children get sufficient sleep, you should establish a bedtime routine and reduce stimulating activities in the night. Also, make their bedroom dark and quiet as it helps to enhance the quality of their sleep. Some children and young ones go on the phone and games at night or wake to it at midnight when adults are sleeping. So watch out in their rooms. If they have to give a response to every text message they get, however good they feel about it, this could become addictive, and not very helpful. It is very crucial to find the correct balance of technology in the household, and proper boundaries and rules can help you as a parent achieve them.

84. Focus on the process, not the result.

Parents who have a habit of overemphasising achievements are likely to raise children with psychological problems. Instead of focusing on achievements, consider focusing on the process. Children who focus on attitude and effort and not the result end up achieving success at the end of the day. So, be on the watch for opportunities to acknowledge the effort, attitude and good behaviour of your children; you'll see that they will achieve great success naturally.

Many people think they'll have a skill when they grow up. A skill doesn't just sprout, it involves a process. The process of getting things done is much more important than the result. The process is what gives a good result. The process is what leads to the discovery of new ideas. The changes you expect will come during the process. Things do not only change during the process, but the process also changes you as well. It allows you to grow. The real changes you experience in terms of development are what make you the person you are, so it's much more beneficial that your skill doesn't just sprout from nowhere.

Ali's aunt, Allison would make him clean the floor again and again, repeating the process until he got it just right. He hated it and used to get angry. "I have done it," he would say, "what is the sense in doing all these many times. " He did not understand the process of excellence. Without the means of diligence, there is no excellence, and without the means of excellence there is no reward or reward is cheap, or you are not well rewarded, your effort is not highly valued.

Ali later had someone in his life who insisted on perfection, who valued process in getting things done. He remembered his aunt and began to appreciate her insistence on the process. It had inadvertently instilled in him the sense of quality and excellence which determined the high value of his excellent work and services.

The process is essential, it makes things work and teaches how to make things. Without process end products lose their value, and they become cheap. People with lousy quality don't have class. By focusing on just result, they groom the terrible attitude of not valuing and respecting the process in what they do. They could be useful, but do not pay attention to detail. The detail is important. Whatever you do, pay attention to the process because it determines the value, cost and price your result attracts.

Charity's mum does not just give her a clean room, she makes her go through the process. Providing a cleanroom is giving the result, but she makes her daughter go through the process of getting the cleaning skill so that she would have the skills, but not without the process. By process, Charity comes to acquire the needed skills.

Charity has the skill to write, so dad asked her to help edit his book, and she gets the money she needed to get some extras. That skill was a result of the process. It always pays. You go through a process of four years to acquire B. sc, and the degree is yours. But if someone gives you the certificate, they have not helped you. You have the license, but without process you have not acquired the skill the document represents. It is the process that makes you skilful. The method of learning is what changes your value and character; and that is what you needed and got.

When you give money to kids for doing nothing, you are not helping them. They will accuse and blame you in future when they lack needed skills. They accuse you because you did not allow them to go through the process. You pay the price for them and shield them from process and change that should happen to them, and they remain who they are and come back and stab you. Process changes your mindset and makes you grow. During the procedure you learn endurance, and endurance gives you stamina. The method also gives you inner content and forms you into a person of value. The technique of failing and getting up changes and makes you a better person.

Process changes you and brings the best out of you. The process will discover your weakness and make you a better person. If you give your children things without process they will abuse it. The method teaches you self control and makes you value little things. The process develops prudence and frugality. It does not focus on the end result. Even in working free, you gain more in the process. We must not cut corners, follow due process.

Physical things are liable to change; it is the invisible things that are not liable to change because they are more stable and predictable. The process goes with values, diligence, responsibility, truth, sincerity, faithfulness and honesty; all great benefits to be taught. They are things that are invisible but sustainable for the future. Your children may fail or make mistakes, but in the process they will begin to do well. Without process values are lost, and everything collapses in time. Of course things collapse when they lack skeleton, anchor or structure that will hold them together. If children don't have these values, they will behave according to whatever situations dictates around them, and that's like leaving things to chance. That's not the right way to live.

85. Give your children more time to play.

By play, I do not mean iPad or arcade games. No. I'm talking about outdoor games; that is, unstructured playtime. Unstructured playtime is essential for the growth and development of a child. It makes their brain relax, gives them a good mood and helps to develop them socially. It gives them time to unplug from the technology that surrounds them.

86. Reduce TV time for your children.

A study of over 4,000 teenagers showed that teenagers who watch TV more were found to become depressive. Make yourself an example for your kid by reducing your own TV time. You can discuss with your kid to decide on the guidelines for watching TV. Set boundaries to provide your child with structure. Within these boundaries, discuss when to watch TV, when to eat and undertake other chores. Get your kids to do so many things that they would spend less time watching TV, lest the habit becomes addictive. Many parents want to get the children off their back and put on the TV in front of them, making the children get their values from there. This escapist option is not as helpful as such parents may think.

Agree that TV time is not exactly controlled or monitored but give alternatives, like cleaning the house, doing repair work, reading a book or sharing an interest that would produce a better result. Children want to express themselves, and when there is no avenue to express themselves they go to games. Negotiate with them the number of hours to be spent on games every day.

87. Motivate your children to keep a gratitude journal.

Studies have shown that keeping a current gratitude journal helps to increase the level of happiness. How can you start a routine of keeping a gratitude journal?

Step 1: Get a pen and a notebook and place them on your bedside table.

Step 2: Make it a habit of writing down the things you are thankful for before you sleep.

Here are some things you can be contented about:

- Optimum health,
- Beautiful sunset,
- Living family,
- Delicious steak for dinner,

- Loving friends.

88. Afford your children the chance to make their own choices.

Children who are allowed to set their own goals and plan their schedules are likely to be focused and disciplined; such children make wise decisions in the long run. Also, let your children choose their desired punishment. Studies have shown that children who do so do not break the rules on purpose. As your children grow older, give them the freedom to make choices and pick activities. This will make them successful and happier. "Compared to adolescents, children's goals and aspirations are characterised as ambitious and unrealistic, and have rarely been considered. Aspirations are related to self-esteem and control beliefs, which are more likely for younger children to be free of societal opportunities and constraints. Therefore, at younger age aspirations may be a better reflection of children's hopes for the future" [24]. No matter what age your child is, remind them of the goals and dreams they have told you about and make them more motivated and inspired to do what they need to in order to make them happy right now, whether their goals are the same or not.

Plan the work to be done with your children, even if things don't work as planned. It is better to have a pre-plan than not doing anything. Do something every day towards your purpose.

For Ages 4-5, tell the child what is to be done and give options to choose. Ask for their interest. Do you want them to draw or read, provide the options with the child so he can choose from. This will help them learn to make choices. Explain why you are doing what you are doing to avoid the child from getting angry and frustrated. Help them participate in deciding things that pertain to them, this way they gain your respect because it shows you respect them and treat them as partners.

89. Settle the conflicts in your marriage.

Children who are products of unsettled homes are likely to drink and abuse drugs. They perform woefully at school, and are likely to develop emotional problems. An unsettled home affects children negatively. They become less engaged, less responsible, less motivated; the situation could cause their health and wellbeing to depreciate over time. If you have long-standing issues in your marriage, please do not hesitate to seek help from a qualified counsellor. Remember, your marriage and children depend on you.

90. Teach your children to be generous and serve others.

How can your children serve others? Children can serve others by volunteering, helping the family, helping their friends and making a difference in society. Children who serve others feel as if they have a meaningful life, and this makes them happy. Another thing that makes children happy is generosity. Kids are delighted when they are able to help others. So, motivate your children to serve others and be generous.

For instance, Kelly and his father went shopping in the supermarket. At the mall, Kelly met a young boy about his age crying. Kelly's dad asked of his parent. The small boy pointed to a short middle-aged man talking to the cashier. Then, Kelly's dad asked why he was crying. He said his father promised to buy him a wristwatch if he had good grades in his exam and he did. When they got to the supermarket, he knew his father does not have the money to buy him a wristwatch. Kelly, without thinking twice, removed the wristwatch his mum got him for his eleventh birthday which he celebrated the past month and stretched it to the boy.

The boy looked at Kelly, then at the wristwatch, but did not take it.

"Don't you like it?" Kelly asked.

"Yes, I do, but it's yours. "

"Don't worry, you can have it. "

"Really? Are you serious?"

"Yes, please. I have another one at home. "

The boy then took the wristwatch happily, and ran to his father. Both father and son came to Kelly and his father. The boy's father, almost in tears, thanked Kelly and his father. The boy and his father left the supermarket happily.

"Why did you do that?" Kelly's dad asked him as soon as the boy and his dad left.

"Nothing, I just felt that I needed to help the boy. He was crying and I couldn't bear that," Kelly said unflinchingly.

I can imagine the excitement on Kelly's dad's face. I have the instinct that Kelly learnt from his parents. Over time, by setting positive, giving examples for their children, parents can help mould their young adult into well-rounded individuals. Just like in this scenario, I bet that you will be surprised just how much your child has been learning just from watching you.

91. Emphasise the utmost importance of a healthy body image.

A healthy body image is expedient for girls in particular, though it's important for boys too. Here are a few ideas on promoting healthy body image in your children:

- Rather than focus on how exercise affects appearance, focus on the health benefits that exercise provides.
- You should concentrate on the development of skills,

career development, physical appearance and character in your children.

- Workout as a family.
- Communicate with your children on how social media affects how we perceive our bodies.
- Do not talk about the guilty feelings that come from eating certain foods.
- Avoid passing negative judgments on the appearance of other people.
- Encourage healthy eating around the home through prepared meals and snacks.
- Hunger is a signal that notifies you that your body needs food. However, it's not telling you to eat anything, it wants you to eat well, working towards a balanced diet. Analyse the food to eat, food that heals and nourishes the body.
- Instinct, stimuli and our reflexes are part of the signs that we are alive. Hunger is an instinct given to man. If you do not have that instinct, you might forget to feed your body. Hunger keeps you living because if you don't have a craving you might not eat; and one may die. Eating instinctively means you are eating because you are hungry; but you should eat what makes you healthy, strengthens and builds you up. If you eat the wrong food, it could lead to poor health in your future, even though you are living and feel okay for now, and may not sense anything is amiss. Analyse food and decide what is good to eat and not what to eat. "Children need regular meals and snacks to get the energy (calories) and goodness or 'nutrients' they need for growing and fighting off illness. Children's nutritional needs change as they get older, so it is vital to be aware of these changes" [25].

92. Don't shout at your children.

You'd be surprised at how yelling or shouting at your children can turn your home into a battleground. Children who are constantly yelled at or children who live in an unfriendly environment are likely to feel anxious and insecure. If your child upsets you so much that you are almost losing your temper, take a walk for ten minutes to gather your thoughts; when you come back, you'll find that you are in control and can now speak to your child in a calm manner.

Mrs Joseph has three teens who get her upset all the time; and in her anger, she shouts and says to the first: "You are good for nothing. " But that sort of statement is the most dangerous thing to say to young people. It damages the emotions and self-esteem of the child and makes the child less likely to come to you in times of need.

Parents/carers are not to provoke their children to anger. Too much control of teens ruins relationship; they want to feel your trust. Rather than control your teens, speak more in discussion and suggestions. Appeal to their understanding, explain things to them always and let them have insight into things as they are. Excessive control hardens the heart of children and turns their heart against parents. You make them hostile if you don't explain things to them. "Make a conscious effort to be aware of how many times a day you say "No" and the reasons why you seem to start all your sentences this way, and then see if you can find another way to redirect your child" [26].

Children see excessive control in the same way they see bullying. When a son/daughter is bullied by his/her father, it might stay with them for the rest of their life. You might also destroy the psyche of the child. Freely change with a changed attitude towards your children. Overreacting parents push their children away; they see their dad, not as a disciplinarian, but a bully.

Chris, a mid-forties parent to Luke, aged 13, told of how his son became detached from his family in particular ways. Chris admitted that he was overbearing; he was technophobic, so each time he would see Luke using a digital device, it would irritate him to the point where he couldn't keep his opinion to himself. Rather than guiding, he would command Luke to come off the digital devices and force him to spend time with his family. The only thing was, this pushed Luke even further away. He may have been there in the room with his family, but emotionally he was disconnected.

At age 12-17, when puberty starts, teens want to find themselves, not according to what their parents have told them but what they come to discover by themselves. They doubt and question everything they have been taught. They want to demonstrate their freedom and liberty, so they are constantly looking for an opportunity to be who they are. They want their freedom which brings about disagreements with parents. They disregard parents authority, and some parents who know what is right, but are not prepared, react irrationally.

Parents must act maturely at this time and be prepared for this change in their teens' behaviour. "The changes in how adolescents think, reason, and understand can be even more dramatic than their obvious physical changes. From the concrete, black-and-white thinkers appear to be one day, rather suddenly it seems, adolescents become able to think abstractly and in shades of grey. They are now able to analyse situations logically in terms of cause and effect and to entertain hypothetical situations and use symbols" [27].

Parents must be less rigid, lessen rudeness in their teens, who want to find themselves, by themselves, and demonstrate their uniqueness. They tend not to respect the authority of parents as they do the opinion of their friend and people outside the family, teachers, magazine and other sources of advice. It is a period they exhibit a rebellious character. Yet, the parent should hear and listen to them. Teens tend to retreat into themselves and not talk to you as much as they used to. They withdraw and do what they want, paint their room, do things that are difficult to explain.

It is a time they doubt themselves and doubt whether they are beautiful. They suspect their natural look and are not sure if they are handsome. Some think they are not normal, too short, or too slim. They question everything about their life and lack confidence and experiment with hairstyles. At puberty, teens tend to copy people they consider superstars on TV, give in to new identity, look for love, any expression of love from peers, and become vulnerable to falling into wrong companies. They think they have been deprived of freedom, so they want all the freedom and liberty they want. They may want to try drinking, experiment with sex. Also at puberty, teens are full of complaints: "Why am I so tall? Why is my hair not gorgeous?" They also want to insist that their opinion is taken.

What should parents do about the changes in their teen's behaviours? Pay attention and be patient. Listen more. Try to be a friend. Talk to them as one equal to another. Treat them as one adult with another. Welcome them. Win their confidence. Show they are loved. Go with them to a café or restaurant. Allow them to practice new things. Make them join theatre groups and be actively involved in the production. Ask direct questions, so they are not embarrassed. Don't push them to answer the questions; show you are interested in their well being.

Create excitement and exciting ambience around them. Take them to shop. Apply fewer laws and rules; teens don't like routines. They hate rules and don't like to be driven and commanded around. They want to be given more freedom. Help them find interesting things and hobbies that truly engage them. Register them at such clubs for photography, writing, video shooting, or whatever they find exciting. Arrange these, so they fall into the right company. Sleepover is an excellent opportunity to find out the right people who are real and constructive. And very importantly, don't stop your teens from talking. Let them speak their mind. Allow them to say what they want. Do more of discussion than instruction, so you don't lose control.

93. Teach your children the act of forgiveness.

According to Dr Martin Seligman, the renowned father of positive psychology, forgiveness is an important driver of happiness in children. Children who are taught the act of forgiveness can turn the negative feelings and experiences of the past to a positive one. This driver increases other satisfaction and happiness levels. For this, be the model your children can emulate. Resolve all personal conflicts.

Teach your children the seriousness of forgiveness and they will make forgiveness a lifestyle. You can't claim you want your children to forgive others and here you recall to them what Mr Band did to you last month and what Mrs Wells did to you last year. You have to be the model that you want your children to become; otherwise, they will never learn to act the way you want them to.

94. Encourage your children to think positively.

Children who are optimistic are happier. Besides encouraging your children to write and keep a gratitude journal, there are other ways to teach your children to embrace positive thinking:

- Have a positive attitude yourself.
- Do not make a mountain out of a molehill. For instance, do not make a broken plate or a spilt drink a big deal.
- Reduce complains.
- Observe the good in others and appreciate them.
- Don't gossip.
- Teach your children to confess positive self-statements that help build confidence and high self-esteem.

95. Create a family mission statement.

Create a family mission statement that describes the collective vision and values of your family. Your family should have a mission statement just like every organisation.

96. Designate a regular time for family meetings

Designate a regular time for family meetings; it could be once a week, and no more than 20 minutes. You can ask your family members questions at the meeting. Here are examples of questions to ask:

- What did you do in the week gone?
- What did you do wrong in the past week?
- What are your plans and objectives for the coming week?
- What is one thing you liked that happened in the last week?

Family planned meetings will help to bring your family closer. Children must be raised intentionally and assembled by laws and principles. Have the right time daily to form and create meaningful impacting discussions that instil in your kids the values you will like to see in them. Parenting is to nurture a child to his fullness of a complete person, not just giving them what to eat and wear. Great and significant as these responsibilities are, merely buying suitable dresses for your kids, ensuring they have a good education and feeding them well. Parenting is much more.

"Family meetings are a structured discussion that can help family anger decrease. Families can use these discussions to resolve specific conflicts that might have just been argued about in the past. Families might use these meetings to discuss issues such as, house rules, vacation plans, sibling rivalry, changes in the family structure" [28].

97. Share your family history and values with your children.

Children who are familiar with the history of their parents tend to have a high level of self-esteem. Sharing your history with your children will help to foster the family bond and make your children resilient.

98. Create family rituals.

Family rituals go a long way in increasing the cohesiveness of a family and developing children socially. Here are some family ritual ideas to create:

- Go for evening walks.
- Have a good breakfast together as a family every Sunday.
- Cook dinner together as a family every Saturday.
- Hold a weekly family meeting.
- Have a family game night.
- Go camping once a year.

99. Find a mentor for your children.

No doubt, you are a mentor for your children. But having another trusted adult to mentor your children will make them more responsible and successful. You can ask a trusted friend to take up the role. As your children grow up, they will make suggestions, listen to them and use their ideas to help them grow. This will help them see things that you have not been able to see; and this would help with skills and knowledge in certain areas of interest.

100. Consistency

Be consistent with your kids; reward or punish the behaviour displayed by your kids in the same manner. When your children do something you said you were going to punish them for, follow through with it. Don't use fear and threat as factors in their upbringing. Fear will stop them from daring, and deny them the confidence they need to go forward. Such concern could dominate and captivate them. It could prevent them from paying the price for advancement because there is fear in their subconscious mind. If you are mean with your kids, they will be withdrawn, become timid and have anger issues. Never bully or terrorise a child.

101. Agree with your kids on the desirable and non-desirable behaviours.

Also, agree on how to reward desirable behaviour and how to punish undesirable behaviour. Reward patience, kindness, calm response to harsh behaviour by others.

These skills set will no doubt, take some time to develop. The key is to start early; then patiently stay on it.

8

GOOD HYGIENE HABITS

No doubt, a lot of teens are affected by the sweaty sock syndrome. Being a teacher, I walk into the examination room and I'm often welcomed by an overpowering smell, so much that I want to leave the door open. The moment a child approaches puberty period, hormones begins to flow, and the hygienic requirements change in some ways. It's important to talk about hygiene in children, but I've seen some parents avoiding the subject.

Some parents think that a 10- or 11-year-old child will learn hygiene tips somewhere or somehow. This isn't true. As a parent, you must teach your son/daughter hygiene tips, not to assume they will discover themselves. Children with poor or dirty hygiene habits are prone to illnesses and diseases; as such, they face unfavourable conse-quences. These children may develop infections and rashes and may even be tagged as dirty at school.

Need I mention that this sort of bad reputation is hard to erase; and it lowers the self-esteem of such a child? So, as a parent/carer, the onus is on you to teach your children the simple hygiene tips and basics. This begs the interesting question of where to start; how can you teach your preteen and teen daughter or son how to take responsibility for hygiene? How can you get your teenage son to shower daily without endless nagging? This chapter will answer these hygiene questions, plus more, and will show you how to teach your children hygiene tips.

When it comes down to hygiene tips, there are quite several things you need to discuss with your children:

102. Showering

Some kids in the elementary classes do not shower every day. In fact, this might not be so noticed for one day; but with more days this becomes obvious. This is expected to change when children approach puberty, and that's when showering daily becomes even more important. Teach your kids to wash their faces, feet, hands, bottoms, and groins with a mild soap. Also, they should clean their fingernails and beneath the nails as well.

103. Hair washing

Sit your children down and discuss the advantages and disadvantages of everyday hair washing. While some teens prefer to wash their hair frequently to prevent hair drying, other teens prefer to wash theirs daily, especially if the hair is an oily one that can cause acne. If your teen girl is having a difficult time with her hair, you could help do research and find the possible things she could use.

104. Application of antiperspirant or deodorant

Before puberty, your child has a lot of working sweat glands. When puberty approaches, the sweat glands are more active, and the chemical makeup of the glands sees some changes that cause them to produce a strong smell. When this happens, introduce antiperspirant or deodorant. These should become a part of your teen's daily hygiene. Bear in mind that some teens who are self-conscious have a twisted or biased perception of how much they sweat. These teens are convinced that they sweat more than their friends, so you need to reassure them.

105. Changing clothes

Before puberty, your child may be used to wearing the same socks, underwear or shirt constantly without others noticing. This changes when he/she approaches puberty. Teach your teen about the need to wear clean clothes and change clothes daily. Teach your kid that showering daily, and changing clothes are an essential part of good hygiene. You should also mention that cotton clothes absorb sweat better.

106. Doubt

Don't sow the seed of suspicion; otherwise, your teen will begin to suspect your motive. This could lead to accusations. People who have suspicion don't have facts. Suspicion destroys the family. It brings strain, anger and breakdown in the relationship. Ask your children question and clear doubts in things you are not sure about. One legacy you want to give to your children is trust. "A breach of trust usually happens when you've given your child some responsibility, freedom or privilege that he misuses or abuses. While your first reaction might be one of anger and betrayal, it's important to remember that this is really not about you. Even though it often feels personal, it's not a reflection on you or your parenting" [29]. Unless you have reason to, you need to have faith in them.

Trust and doubt work both ways too. Don't build false hope or dash their hopes. If you say you are going to Disney land and you did not do it, it affects the psyche of the child; or you promise the child could have sleepover when you know you won't let him go, then you say: "Next time," yet again, you disallow him/her; the first signal of lack of trust is that the child stops reminding you. The child has concluded you can't be trusted with your words. Whereas your promises ought to inspire your children and give them hope, your words are making them frustrated instead. Then you ruin your relationship because trust is broken. Tell your children and explain why you did not do what you promised, call and apologise to them. They will appreciate that. But when you lie to them, they begin to lie too, and won't see anything wrong doing so. A student once told me, Miss, don't believe my mum- She is a liar.

107. Preventing acne

From age 10, your child should develop the habit of washing the face twice a day. While most kids do not have acne breakout out at that age, it's smart and essential to start the habit of face washing early. Ensure you teach your child not to wash the face vigorously as that will leave the skin irritated and cracked.

108. Hair removal and shaving

When you spot hair on the legs of your daughter or on the upper lip of your son, you can introduce them to razor use. Now, your child may not want to start shaving yet, but you would have done your duty as a parent. Introduce your teen girls to hair removal products. You. uld help buy a shaving product and walk them through how to use it. For example, teaching the teenage son how to shave in front of the mirror while his father does the same can prove to be a valuable bonding moment.

109. Keeping good oral health

Teens may be a bit unconcerned about their oral hygiene, so you need to teach them that flossing, and brushing are expedient, especially if they fancy drinking sports drinks, sugary drinks and coffee. Besides causing tooth decay, bad oral hygiene causes bad breath. No teen wants bad breath.

"Hey, Mary, I bought you a new toothbrush. You've been using your toothbrush close to three months I suppose. You need to change it. " Information like this helps the teen to know when to change the toothbrush and how to have good oral hygiene in general.

110. Understanding the body

If you are teaching your teen on good hygienic, you should also talk about puberty. Your teen girls need to know about menstruation and breast development. Likewise, your teen boys need to know about wet dreams and erections. Do not just brush over these topics, discuss them extensively. If you do not teach them these topics, you can be sure they would get the untrue version from their peers. Give your teen a book that addresses the topics or refer them to a health website that addresses the topics, and then help them answer any questions they have about their bodies if they ask.

In dealing with teen hygiene myths, we do not only talk about the benefits of good hygiene, we should also talk about unimportant things. During their teen years, teenager's knowledge of how the body works is riddled with myths and misconceptions. Here are some of the typical teen hygiene myths:

- Shaving makes the hair grow thicker and faster.
- Oily foods cause the breakout of acne.
- A tan is a cure for acne

These are what they are: myths. And you should tell your girl to doubt or question whatever her friends tell her. You'll be surprised at how teens quickly believe bizarre things.

111. Teen practice of good hygiene

Most kids listen to advice about good hygiene because they have fixed interest and do not want to be tagged the dirty kid. They never want to have terrible acne, so they shower daily and practice good hygiene because the last thing they wish is to be made fun of at school. On the other hand, peer pressure does not allow some teens to practice good hygiene. I find teen boys more prone to poor hygiene habits.

When it comes to teaching teen boys good hygiene, extra measure needs to be taken. Some teen boys do not care. They do not want to shower even after a workout session. As such, they smell bad and may soon start developing infections, rashes and other problems. Here are a few useful hints to get your teen to learn proper hygiene habits.

112. Make practising good hygiene a responsibility.

If you find that your teen is reluctant and doesn't want to learn basic hygiene, he or she doesn't shower daily and doesn't even use antiperspirant or deodorant, you need to make good hygiene a responsibility. Sit them down and expound to them that caring for oneself is a responsibility, and they should take it like other household chores. Just as they are expected to take the trash out, tidy and clean their rooms, they are also expected to look after their hygiene.

Now, after making it a responsibility and the child still isn't receptive, make him/her know that there are repercussions for their behaviour. The consequences may be revoked privileges. However, rather than continually criticising and are never satisfied with their efforts and complain about insignificant things, begin to acknowledge them in the process of the good they have done. Don't reject their attempt, which annoys them, and the conflict starts. Take your cool and don't be reactionary while you are red hot. "As children reach puberty, and their bodies change, their cleaning habits need to change with them" [30]. Help them to understand that whilst not embarrassing them and ensure both child and parent are approaching the topic with the most rational mindset.

Avoid shouting and scream. Acts like this leave traces in the minds of young, impressionable children, which may end them up shouting as well. Walkout. Let your emotion go down before you talk. Respond instead of reacting. It is counterproductive when you use anger to correct children. Correct them, but not in anger or when you are furious because they don't feel your love at such a moment. Correct your children in love. Express love in 10 ways before you can correct once.

113. Begin early.

Most parents start teaching their children good hygiene at age 10. Don't come too hard on them. Do not begin by belittling your child about their hygiene. Refrain from confronting them, and don't make it a struggle; otherwise, your child will dig in his or her heels. Ensure that you provide up to date information. Before you start teaching your kids about good hygiene, you want to be sure that you know what you are talking about. Learn the necessary information, double-check since some of the tips you adopted growing up may now be outdated.

114. Be a great role model yourself.

Before you start teaching your child about good hygiene, you want to be sure that you practice good hygiene. Don't make your child see you in pyjamas now and then; the child will do same or even worse, as some children cannot be bothered to put in any effort or give the minimum to changing into the right clothes. Your kid will not brush his teeth if he has never seen his mother brush before.

Why leave food sediments in your mouth into the next meal when you can do a thorough mouth wash after every meal? It's not only a bad example to leave a child, but it also portrays the parent as a bad coach. The minimum oral hygiene should be to brush twice, first in the morning and before you retire to bed at night.

115. Pair up.

If you are a mother, talk to your teen daughter about proper hygiene and have the father talk to the son too. Teaching kid's good hygiene is better practised when there's a same-sex parent (father/son and mother/daughter) to talk about these issues with the child. Children tend to look up to a mother or father as a model for hygiene.

This creates a bond and enhances the relationship in the teen's life as they may be finding trouble with friendships at school or other places outside of the home.

116. Seek professional backup

If after teaching your child proper hygiene they still can't learn the subject, make an ally of a paediatrician. You can ask a paediatrician to reinforce some hygiene issues before the next appointment.

Talking to Your Kids on Teen Hygiene: when you are teaching and encouraging your child to practice good hygiene, you are expected to explain the context of good hygiene. Explain why good hygiene isn't a set of rules that you are enforcing on them, and help them understand why good hygiene is something they should want to achieve. Teens need to be well versed with the subject of taking care of themselves as they are close to adulthood. In the coming years, they will start building relationships with the opposite sex or having a roommate, at which time good hygiene matters.

Empathise with your teen! Remember that the period of puberty is confusing, and your teen will have some questions about hygiene that he/she doesn't know answers too. So, try to give space for your teen to ask questions. Don't be surprised that they may not welcome your attempt to talk about hygiene; they may even roll their eyes, protest and insist that they are not interested. Keep teaching them; do what you have to do, and in the long run they'll be grateful you did.

9

TIME MANAGEMENT AND ORGANIZATIONAL SKILLS

Are you an exhausted parent fed up with reminding, prodding and poking your teen to finish chores and homework on time? Do you go crazy merely looking at the chaos in the backpack of your child? Well, you are not alone. To change behaviour, you should not start with teaching a strategy or a skill. No. You need to understand the brain first. The challenges of your child and teen are seated in their brain development, majorly in the section of the brain at the back of the forehead. There you find the neuron networks that are connected to organisation and time management.

According to neuroscientists, organisation and time management are two major executive functions of the brain. Your teen has challenges with time management and organising binders because the executive functions of the brain are the last part to develop. Usually as parents and teachers, we expect our children, teenagers and young adults to act like adults when it comes to organisation and time management. But you can't force your child and teen's brain to do what the brain cannot do. Don't be in a rush, or worry when their organisational standards are not up to yours. The maturing of this part of the brain could take years, and can even extend into college years. I had seen cases of people who entered well into their twenties before they developed into functioning adults in terms of full brain functionality.

What can you do as a parent? How can you help your child and teen develop time management and organisational skills? To start, you need to stop apportioning blame on your child. If your child's brain cannot deal with time internally, then as a parent, you need to provide support for the brain externally with strategies and tools to keep track of time. Also, you should teach your child time management and organisational skills carefully and thoughtfully. You can get it done. Here are things you should do:

117. Teach your child to estimate time.

Most children aren't even aware of the time it takes to get a task done, hence, they delay starting chores or completing their homework. They assume that time can be stretched. So, when they have to do an unpleasant task, they assume that the task is time-consuming, and instead of getting right into it, they opt to have fun first to avoid the task. Of course, the things children enjoy, such as YouTube, video games and Snapchat, make time go fast; and a little time spent on these activities can accumulate into a lot of time. Before you and your child know it, deadlines approach and what could have been handled days ago is now being rushed in a matter of hours.

The solution to this is to build your child into a time scientist. You need to teach them to collect data for the time a particular task takes to accomplish, from start to finish. Design a record sheet for the simple activities your child does, and then include a breakdown of his morning routines, chores and homework subjects. The record sheet should have two columns, with one serving for the time your child estimates to finish the tasks, and the second recording the actual time it took to get the task done.

In the instance where your child insists on multitasking while doing homework, create a time record which compares the time needed to finish the homework with multitasking and without multi-tasking.

To get the full benefit of this activity, start by timing a couple of activities daily and make sure to talk about the results. You should ask your child what he noticed and what surprised him about the time the task took as opposed to his estimated time. Building your child into a time scientist and making him/her collect data will make them more realistic about the time it takes to finish activities, thereby making them plan better. They'll find that doing homework and chores takes less time than they estimated once they remove distractions. This knowledge opens the way for time management, the value of work and the value of time; not how hard you work, but how diligent.

118. Teach your teen how to make a plan.

Children and teens tend to live just in the now; they do not really consider the future. They want to have fun at the moment and push work till later. But this often results in conflicts with algebra and melt-down before sleeping. To avoid this, teach your child and teen to create a to-do list and daily plan. Here's how to teach your kid the planning process:

- Offer your kid a tool to write down the plan. Consider providing a small whiteboard and make sure the board is kept in the sight of your kid while he's doing homework.

- Fix a routine time to plan. Making a plan needs to be a regular habit, so routine is an important word here. Simply create a routine by connecting a new habit with an old one. For instance, snack time after school hours is a great time to plan for the rest of the evening.

- Show your child the plan-making process. You can do this by scribbling down your plan for the day. Your goal is to model the plan-making process. Write out all the activities and chores you need to do from morning until the end of the day.

- Teach your child to write his/her plan. Do not do it for them. When the teaching is still fresh and early, instruct your child to check the planner and copy out the assignments that are due. Even if the tasks are given online, your child should still write it in one place. If he is confused about homework, have him contact a classmate, or the teacher to get rid of the confusion. Your child's plan should include family chore, a responsibility at home, school projects, homework and after-school activities as well as a fun thing to do after accomplishing the tasks to give them something to strive towards.

- Note the time it takes your child to get each task done on the list.

- Reinforce your child to rule out tasks after completion as the brain loves the feeling that comes after completing a task. This positive feeling encourages the child to take on the next task.

- Instruct your child to show you the completed task once done. While this isn't a part of the planning, it helps to build accountability by showing that the task is done. You need not correct it, just check that it's completed and praise your child.

Teaching your child the planning process helps him/her to develop the habit of getting tasks done on their own. Planning is the bedrock of time management.

119. Use the analogue clock.

Do you find that your teen spends longer time than required on homework or a task because he/she was daydreaming, multitasking or avoiding the task? One particular reason why this happens is that children and most adults cannot track how time passes in their mind. They try but they are lost in time, not sure if time is moving forward while they remain in the present.

The solution to this challenge is to use an analogue clock and place it in the sight of the child while he's doing homework. An analogue clock is preferable to a digital clock because the former shows the present moment of time using both past and future. An analogue clock shows how long a child has been working, that is the past; and the time he/she has left to get the task done, and get on to the next one, that is the future.

Keeping an analogue clock in the sight of your child will help them calculate progress against the time available to work. As they see the hands of the clock move forward, they are geared to finish the task by the deadline.

120. Do use monthly calendars.

Does your teen consistently wait until the last minute before working on assignments or projects? Does this dragging result in an emotional outburst between your child and you? Does the dragging results in low quality work or lower grades as a result of missed deadlines and assignments that wasn't submitted? Again, the root of this problem is traced back to the brain of young teens that live just in the present, and cannot see the big, long term picture.

I've encountered students who can only track the assignments that are due in the next couple of hours or days. They couldn't grasp the assignments that will be delivered at a later date. They tend to think that they have ample time to work on the task, so they start procrastinating. Before they know it, the future arrives without notice. Suddenly, the deadline that was still far ahead is now two days. To resolve this challenge, you need to teach your child to see the future; and there's no better tool to use than a monthly paper calendar.

Keep the calendar within reach. Train the child to put exams, projects or assignments that are due at a later date on the calendar. I advise that you train your child to make crossing off each day at the end of the day a daily ritual. Seeing the future in this light will help to develop planning skills in your child. The ability to plan and execute a project before the deadline is a crucial life skill for adults. You can start to train your child now to form a connection with the future.

121. Keep a family calendar.

With an accessible calendar, monitor the activities of each member of the family. Motivate your teen to write down his/her entries and use the calendar as a reference when making plans. You may check the schedules and update the calendar together as a family over breakfast.

122. Introduce checklists.

The checklists can be as simple as "What to take along on vacation" or "The things to do before hitting the bed. " Creating lists together helps greatly in developing the ability of your teen to plan tasks and organise his/her time.

123. Designate chores that involve categorising or sorting.

Sorting photos, cleaning the closet, shopping for grocery, emptying the dishwasher and other chores that allow your teen to make lists, plan and arrange things are great choices. You will find it surprising that your teen finds it interesting and as well begins to learn faster. Your teen will also feel a great sense of achievement when he or she completes the task.

124. Get set the night before.

While this may be a tough one for both of you, it sure does the work if you can develop the habit. You might be very tired because the day was long; but at the same time, it is of much importance that you make sure your teen is ready for whatever ought to be done the next day. If he/she is going to school, make sure they did all their assignments or projects, their clothes are neat and ironed, their bags well packed, and all of that. I am not saying you should do it yourself; what I am saying is that you make sure your child does it. It will help prevent rush and unnecessary anxiety and panic the next day; and of course, if it goes on well, it becomes a habit for your teen.

Creating lists and tasks that your teen can do ahead of time creates a young adult that prepares himself or herself and is always ready to do the best they can.

125. Use closet organisers and containers.

Your teen will probably find it much easier to collect items, use, keep neat, and return if there is a container for everything. You should also incorporate pick up time into teen's daily routine. Encourage your teen to find organisational ideas that fit and suit their techniques

126. Get a planner for your child.

Ask the child to pick out the planner that interests him/her, so they can be excited about using it. When you get your teen a planner, it shows him/her that you find their time valuable and you want to encourage them to write a schedule. Make sure to coordinate the information on the planner with the family calendar to avoid conflicts.

127. Organise schoolwork.

Ensure that your child keeps his/her notes, handouts, homework, and assignments in different folders. Make it a habit to check their backpack every night; also set aside a time weekly to check their folders so they learn to become responsible for their academics and organisation.

128. Create a homework routine.

Create a home schedule that allows study hour for your child. Set up an ideal workspace, be it the kitchen table or his/her room. Reinforce your child to adhere to the schedule, and on days when he/she doesn't have homework, they should read, review their notes or solve a crossword puzzle. Be there to support and help your child if they need it, but allow them to attempt the problems by themselves first.

129. Have a homework supply box.

Get a handy box and fill it with school supplies. Encourage your kid to keep pens, measurement tools, calculator and paper in the box, so everything he/she needs will be available at their disposal.

130. Cook together.

Cooking teaches kids to measure, follow directions, separate ingredients and manage time. These are all essential elements in the organisation. Also, have your child help you plan meals and put together a grocery list. Especially your teen, it is important you two get close in the kitchen. He/She might seem a slow cook, but I tell you, he's/she's learning. During the cooking, you can also talk to your teen and let him/her know much about the kitchen and kitchen hygiene.

131. Nurture an interest in collections.

If you sense that your kid has a particular interest, reinforce him/her to develop and organise the collection. The collection could be as simple as cancelled stamps or rocks; she just needs to sort, classify and arrange the collection.

132. Reward your kid and support them with organisational tasks.

Your kid may have an interest in a particular challenge and want to organise. Help him/her develop the routine and laud them for a job beautifully done.

Mother: Hey, Lizzy, remember that excellent article you wrote last year?

Daughter: Yes mum. What happened?

Mother: Well, Franca read it and said you are so good. She asked if you would be interested in joining a group of young writers.

Daughter: Really, mum? Are you serious?

Mother: I told Franca yes, but you would need to speak with her. I will take you tomorrow and you can tell her yourself!

You don't know how elated this kid will be. Seeing her mum support her dream and routine will be the best thing that happened to her, and help her realise the strength of the relationship you share

133. Teach your child how to handle papers

Do you discover that your child or teen lose papers between home and the school? Does your child lose assignments before turning them in? A child with such behaviour simply has a brain that has trouble organising things. To solve this challenge, simply teach your teen the principle of organisation and the importance of staying organised. Teach the child that everything has and needs a home, papers inclusive. Teach the child that each piece of paper he's given at school shouldn't be stuffed in a backpack or a binder; it should be kept in just one location.

You need to teach your child the two steps for handling school papers. First, your child needs to sort out what to do with the papers that he was given at school, and he needs to figure out how to handle the papers once he gets home. Teachers do not usually hand out papers to students at the right time; they hand out the pile of papers when the child wants to get on a bus or when he's rushing to the next class. Because of the time the paper was handed to the child, he/she just stuffs it somewhere, and may not remember when he needs the paper.

The solution is to provide your child with a transparent two-pocket plastic folder. The folder should be placed in front of the child's school binder, so it can be easily accessible. The folder should be the first thing that welcomes your child when he opens the binder. Encourage him/her to keep all papers collected at school in the folder. There is no specific order of arrangement; the child should just keep all the papers in the home folder. On getting home, the child has enough time to organise the papers.

They should empty the folder. Then you should teach them how to organise the mixed pile of papers. As you teach your child the organising skills, each paper will fall into any of these categories:

- **Recycle:** This applies to a paper with no grade signed on it, such as a practice paper. Parents should see this or sign it. Create a space in the house for your child to keep the papers in this category.
- **Pages needed for later use at school**: These might be reference pages, project descriptions or rubrics for grading. These papers should be kept behind the pocket divider of each subject.
- **Store graded papers:** Unless necessary, the child doesn't need to bring graded papers to school every time. Graded papers are kept as an insurance and alternative in the event where the teacher misses record grades accidentally. Provide a file or a box for your child to toss the grades papers in and keep until the grades for the subjects are released before recycling them.

The last step of this paper organising process is to ensure that the child gets the completed assignment to school. Teach your child to keep the finished homework in the home folder but place it in a specific way and place. The completed homework should be kept in the pocket on the left side of the folder. The assignments should be kept face up to enable the child to see them immediately he/she opens the binder. The homework should be kept in the order by which they will be handed in. For instance, if mathematics homework will be handed in first, the English homework should be placed behind the mathematics homework.

Teaching your child this process goes a long way in reducing concern and stress over missing homework or papers. Likewise, there will be an improvement in your child's grade when they learn to manage their papers and assignments. Over time, allow your child to adopt their organisational techniques. Here are some things you shouldn't do:

134. Do not expect your child to be independent very early.

Usually, on the night before starting high school, an authority figure goes before the parents to tell them that the time has come for the children to grow up and assume responsibility. You should step back and give them the reins. This advice is wrong on all levels as it sets a whole lot of children up to fail. By following this advice, you are ignoring what you have learnt about the brain development of teens. The executive functions of teens' brain do not mature fully until they reach the ages of 25-30 years.

Now, the problem is our culture, and the school expects children to be able to use advanced tools to finish the tasks that are expected of adults. The time-consuming activities done after school as well as the demands of several teachers put more pressure on the immature brain of teens. Getting behind in class is very easy; and as a parent, you should remember that you can only do what your brain can do.

Instead of being discouraged, you should change your gears from control to coaching. You want to teach your child organisation and time management skills. You want to support the brain development of your child, and not getting discouraged will help your child to learn how to manage the demands of school.

135. Do not lose your cool.

Avoid saying things like, "Young lady, if you don't drop the video game and do your homework, I'll take away your tablet, phone and computer. " If the behaviour of your child has caused you to yell or talk, then you have experienced what I describe as the emotional control of the brain.

Whenever you feel a strong emotion, anger especially, toward your child, the emotional control of the brain takes over automatically, and you can't access the problem solving, overpowering calm part of the brain. The danger of this loss of control over emotions is that when you lose your cool with someone, you automatically put on the emotional control of their brain and this makes them lose control as well. Before you know what's happening, you both keep pushing your buttons and your brains are soon flooded with chemical hormones that stop you both from thinking calmly and responding calmly. When this happens, things that either one of you says aren't choices made out of reason, they are made out of anger.

What you should know about the emotional centre of the brain is that it cools down very quickly. How? The moment you start feeling frustrated or tension rising, sit down and place your hands behind your neck with your elbows out. Breathe in deeply to push your belly out a bit. Breathe out slowly. Repeat the deep breaths, and as you do, a calming set of chemicals is activated in your brain. Teach your family about the emotional centre of the brain and how to calm down when tension or frustration builds.

136. Never assume that homework is only done in the bedroom.

I remember the first desk I used for my homework. I felt I was a grown-up. The desk was placed in my room where I sit and do my homework. Even before the introduction of technology, distractions like mobile phones and other similar devices and apps, there were a lot of things which I did in my room instead of homework. For most children like me, being left to do homework in the bedroom is not a good idea. Many children do not want to do homework, and for such children, using the bedroom is a bad idea as it takes a mature brain to start tasks you don't have any interest in. It also takes a mature brain to finish the task until it's done.

If you leave your child to do homework alone in their room, chances are you are held down with wishful thinking, imagining that your child is busy doing his/her homework at their desk. If you find that your child cannot work alone in his room, the good way around it is to remove all distractions. You need to create a space with no TVs or background music. It could be on the dining room table where you can have a more careful eye over their work. While your child is working at the end of the table, sit on the other end and keep yourself busy with things you don't have an interest in, such as working on taxes.

Doing this will keep you engaged with two essential things: first, your presence will support your child to put aside distractions and finish the work. Second, you will be a model that shows that even adults sometimes sit down to work on the things they do not have interest in. As your child matures and grows older, you can leave the table, since he/she has mastered the act of working without distractions, and your child will be proud to have earned your trust and will go on to work hard even after you left the table.

137. Never forget to ask about projects.

Has there been a time when your son/daughter announced a big project that is due the coming week or the coming month? A project can cause a problem for children and teens as their immature brain lives in the present. It doesn't think about the future. Their brain interprets projects as something that can be completed far in the future. They do not start working on the project early enough; they wait till the deadline of the project is tomorrow or a few days. The solution to this problem is easy. Simply ask your child if he has projects or homework to work on. Ask about projects regularly; when you do, you are helping your child think about the future. Teach your child to break the project into small steps to meet the deadline.

138. Do not misinterpret confusion.

When you find your child dragging his/her feet or avoiding to start an assignment, your first reaction would be to blame him/her for procrastinating. What many parents do not know is that there are several reasons for procrastination; and they often ignore the cause of the confusion.

The challenge starts the moment a teacher brings a new concept into the picture and the child doesn't understand it. Of course, the child would ask for help in class but before the end of the day, the immediate need for help has disappeared from his brain. When this happens, such a child leaves the classroom confused and hopes that when he gets home the teacher will somehow reappear. Unfortunately, this isn't how it works.

Instead of blaming your child for procrastinating, you can calmly ask if there's anything he's confused about. What the child is confused about maybe as simple as understanding directions or the meaning of new vocabulary. When you help your child clear his confusion, you are also teaching him the importance of asking for help. Embolden your child to ask for help when he's confused.

In summary, do not blame the child, blame the brain. Organisation and time management are executive functions of the brain that take time to develop. So, if you find that your child's brain cannot accommodate something, introduce external supports such as calendars, analogue clock, and making a daily plan for chores and homework.

- Teach your child time and organisation; this includes learning how to calculate the time it takes to accomplish tasks and avoiding distractions to accomplish tasks.
- Provide a home for everything. Being organised starts with providing a home for everything, especially papers got from school.
- Do not rush into blaming your child for his procrastinating behaviour. Be calm and never allow anger to take over. Ascertain if the child is indeed procrastinating or is confused.

Now that you know how a teen's brain works, you can figure out the reason why your teen acts and behaves the way he/she does, thus find it easy to be supportive. Take the time to teach your teen organisation and time management skills. When you do this, the executive functions of their brain will develop, and they will grow up to be the adults of your dreams. Start early and do it little by little. You can do this!

10

HOUSEKEEPING BASICS

As a parent, one of the essential things you can do for your teen is to teach him/her how to develop household cleaning routine. Help your teen to develop habits that will serve him/her throughout adulthood. Bear in mind that teens struggle to remember the things they consider mundane. Still, when they develop a habit, it becomes part of their world. I recommend you start by including tasks in their routine early and a little at a time. Set expectations and give them time to meet your expectations on their own; and when they have learnt the ability to finish a task, assign the child another task.

By the time the child is grown and ready to leave home, they should have learned a lot about the basics of keeping a house clean. I wouldn't want you to think that you are dumping the housework on your teen. Remember that you are grooming him/her to become a successful and independent adult. Give your teen the independence of doing a home management routine while he/she is still under your roof; this way you'd be sure that the habits he/she has developed will keep them going when they leave the house. Ensure that your teen has a basic understanding of the following areas.

139. Set up a regular household cleaning routine.

Teach your teen how to:

- Wash dishes with his/her hands.
- How to use a dishwasher.
- Clean bathrooms, shower, shower doors, sink mirrors, toilets, and floors.
- Use a vacuum cleaner
- Make a bed.
- Dust.
- Pick up clutter.
- Organise a closet.
- Organise drawers.
- Organise paperwork.
- Take out the trash.
- Recycle.

140. Simple household repairs

When the right time comes for your teenager to live in an apartment, a college dormitory or the day when he/she buys a home, they will want to know how to do minor repairs in the home. So, teach your teen how to:

- Paint a room.
- Make a hole in a wall.
- Caulk a bathtub.
- Repair asphalt.
- Repair a screen.
- Weather-strip doors and windows.

- Hang a picture.
- Unblock a gutter.

141. Clothing care

Since your teen wears clothes every day, it's essential that you teach him/her how to keep and care for their clothing. It's normal for the mother/father to buy clothes for the family; this is especially true for mothers who have only boys. However, you need to teach your teen son and daughter how to buy clothes that fit correctly. Also, you need to teach them how to maintain their clothes.

Teach your teen how to:

- Buy clothes.
- Set a budget.
- Find the right fit.
- Know when to buy new items.
- Know the basics to buy – undershirts, socks, jeans, T-shirts, dress clothing, shorts, coats, sportswear, suits, hats, gloves, dresses, and all types of shoes.

142. Laundry care

Laundry is a task that never ends, so it's crucial that you teach your children how to manage their clothing, how to buy, how to replace, how to do laundry, how to iron, how to sew and how to keep clothes when they are still young.

Teach your teen how to:

- Use the washer.
- Use the dryer.

- Use a Laundromat.
- How to hand wash.
- Hang washed clothing to dry.
- Iron clothes.
- Sew a button, mend a tear, and sew and hem.

143. Hanging clothes in a closet

Though hanging clothes in a closet seem like a simple matter for most people, never assume that your teenager knows how to do this. Each item of clothing has a specific technique for hanging.

Teach your teen how to:

- Hang dresses.
- Hang a dress shirt.
- Hang straps.
- Hang a suit.
- Hang winter clothing.
- Hang a collared shirt.
- Hang accessories.

144. How to fold clothes and household items

We all seem to have a specific method for folding T-shirts, towels and jeans. Still, a good rule of thumb will be to teach your teen how to fold clothes. You could teach them how you fold clothes to fit your space, the folding method you learnt from your mother or at the retail clothing store you once worked. Let me give you a little secret; the goal of folding is to fold your clothes to fit your space and to ensure that fresh clothes from the dryer do not wrinkle.

Teach your teen how to fold clothes; but if they have their method, encourage them. Do not make your teen feel like his effort isn't good enough. Do projects together, do events together to give a process of bonding, so that your teens have fun doing it with you.

145. Securing a place to live

Having an abode, dwelling, or a home is one of the necessities of life. It's not just important but crucial to teach your teens how to secure their own space. Getting a home is one of the most significant steps in a person's life, and can be a humongous boost of self-esteem and confidence.

Teach your teen how to:

- Understand background checks.
- Budget for rent.
- Buy house and mortgages.
- Set up and manage utilities.

146. Home mechanical management

Regardless of wherever you live, there are home mechanical management basics that we all need to know how to do, including teens. Teach your teens these skills and have them practice regularly.

Teach your teen:

- Gardening basics.
- Lawn care.
- How to replace a furnace filter.
- Paint walls.
- Unclog a toilet and drain.
- Add salt to the water softener.
- Use the circuit breaker box.
- Turn off water supply lines.

- How to use devices such as a wrench, hammer, screwdriver, and electric screwdriver.

147. Automotive competence

Truth be told, multitasking can be difficult for our teen boys and girls. As such, driving and all the necessities related to car maintenance may be daunting for parents who want to teach them these. Do you know that you can show your teen decision-making skills while you are driving with him/her in the car?

For instance, you are driving with your teen son in the car and it starts raining. When you turn on the headlights, make sure you tell him how you turned it on and why you did it. Tell him you turned the headlight on because it's raining, and you want to make it easier for the oncoming cars to see you. Besides, one of the laws of several counties/states is to turn on the headlights when it's raining. While this is an example, it proves how important and easy it is to help your teen learn simple tasks that they will need to know as they become independent adults.

Another instance is when you pull up in the parking lot and park in a spot. Tell your teen why you parked at the spot. Tell him you parked there because the other spot is narrow, and it makes it hard to drive into. You can further say that the narrowness of the other spot is as a result of the red truck parked closed to the line. Tell him that you could have parked there but you want both of you to be safe, so you opted to choose a wide space. When you inform your teen of the decisions you made at the moment, you are helping them understand the last-minute decisions you make every day.

Teach your teen how to:

- Make decisions.
- Get and renew a driver's license.

- Navigate on the road.
- Read a map.
- Find information.
- Use a navigational app.

Teach your child housekeeping basics so you don't have to worry when they grow into adults and leave the house. Make your child into an independent adult.

11

DEVELOPING SAFETY TIPS

Who is the best person to teach your children and teens safety tips? You! As a parent, you are the best and right person to teach your child personal safety tips.

What are the safety tips for teaching your children?

- Strong character.
- Smart thinking.
- Sticking together.

When should you teach them? As soon as possible! I mean immediately. There is no known regulation that says you should teach your child safety tips at a particular age. However, the ability of a child to understand and practice safety tips is affected by his age, education and developmental levels. And how do you teach your child and teen safety tips?

148. Listen to your children.

- Be familiar with their habits and daily activities.

- Be well versed with the things they like and the ones they do not like.
- Reinforce open communication in the family. Encourage your teen that they can always talk to you about anything.
- Assure your children that their safety is of utmost concern to you.

149. Set boundaries

Set boundaries. Let your children know the places they should go, the kind of people they should see, and the things they should do. Encourage the importance of the friendship system. People they meet and books they read influence their value system. Teach your children always to trust their instincts, and should say no when required.

Conscience is the first voice of God to all humans, and all children have it too. Conscience is a warning sign; it warns us, and children must be taught not to suppress the voice of the conscience. If they do, their conscience will become insensitive, where, when they do a wrong thing the conscience does not prick; the voice of conscience is what tells you when you have done something wrong or veering from the right and appropriate behaviour.

Conscience is the indicator of moral sickness, just like pain informs us that something is wrong in the body. But you must know you are sick before you go to the doctor. So, obeying your conscience is how you set things right. Conscience is the most important thing to develop in all children, and it gets more informed of what is right when we train children to read the book of books – the Holy Bible.

John is a 14-year-old boy who is friends with James and he wanted to go out with his friend to the shopping mall but his mum had warned him to come back at 5 pm. At that time more of their class friends have just arrived at the scene to make it more fun, but he had to obey his mum. So he said bye to his friends and walked to the bus station to stand and wait for the bus home. But after a while, one of his friends ran to him to convince him to stay and find a way of making up a story to his mum.

He stayed and listened to his friend as he wanted the fun of having his friends around as well. But after about two minutes his conscience was pricking him; and he did not want to disobey the gentle voice in him, so he left. His conscience told him to go home, so he did. And on getting home he saw his grandmother on the floor needing help. So he called an ambulance for her. If he had not gone the time he did his grandma could have died. His conscience saved the day. All men must be respected whether they are good or not. What role truth plays in your life determine who you are. Real people respect their conscience. Live by their conscience, honour their conscience. Listen to conscience. Be led by that voice so your conscience is not seared.

150. Be involved.

- Be aware of where your child and teen is at all times.
- Encourage your child to notify you when there are changes in their plans.
- Bear in mind that nothing can substitute your supervision and attention.
- Practice safety tips with your child.
- Let your children know that you are a safe resource and will always be there for them whenever or wherever they are.

Teach your child safety tips over and over again till they become their second nature.

TIPS TO HELP CHILDREN STAY SAFE

151. Encourage your children to know their full name and the home telephone number.

Teach your children how to use the telephone. Make your contact information available to your children; your mobile/cell phone number, paper and office phone number.

152. Trusted Adult

Ensure that you entrust your children to a trusted adult they can call in the case of an emergency.

153. Babysitter

Be vigilant when choosing babysitters. Talk to your friends, neighbours and family members to give you references. After choosing a babysitter, make sure to check in suddenly and unexpectedly to observe how your children are faring. Also, inquire from your children their experience with the babysitter and listen to their responses. Listen to unspoken words in their body language.

SAFETY IN THE NEIGHBOURHOOD

154. Significant landmarks

Sit with your child/children and make a list of the boundaries and choose significant landmarks.

155. Neighbours

Interact with your neighbours regularly and inform your children about the homes they are permitted to visit.

156. Staying close

Do not drop your children alone at movie theatres, malls, parks or video arcades.

157. Be alert

Tell your kids that adults do not ask children for directions or help. Let them know that when an adult approaches them, they should be vigilant.

158. Unknown car

Never leave your child or teen alone in an automobile. Teach your son/daughter not to approach an unknown vehicle.

159. Permission first

Teach your children not to go anywhere without asking for your consent first.

SAFETY AT SCHOOL

160. Beware of abductors

Take precautions when you write your child's name on backpacks, clothing, bicycle license plates or lunch boxes. When your child's name is noticeable, they stand at the risk of being taken by an abductor.

161. Route to school

Walk the path from the school with your child; and while at it, point out the safe places and the landmarks to go when they find that they are being followed by someone or when they need help. Create a map with your child or teen that shows the acceptable routes to school with the main roads. If your children go to school with the school bus, accompany them to the bus stop and ensure that they know the right bus to follow.

LAST WORD

Children learn through practice and what is practised stays in memory to develop the child. Parenting forms values in a child. Children with no values that they have practised throughout their life do not have a backbone or support system to face the world.

Building Confidence

Confidence in children starts with the assessment of other people. If a teacher says to a child, "You are rubbish," a child without engrained values would likely take that literally. But children who are being supported by parents grow friendly and confident, not just mentally; their inner values develop them to become masters of life, not puppets to other people's opinions.

Parent, I urge you to heal the harm individual unguarded carers/teachers have done, so your child would grow confident in himself/herself. Working consistently with children for a longer period regularly helps develop a skill, not just in a couple of days, weeks or even two years. It has to be consistent and regular work; that's how to develop the needed skills to help children grow confident and successful. Sadly, this is where many parents get it wrong. They teach a child once or twice and expect the child to get it. Some training takes 15 to 20 sessions for the child to get it, when they finally wake up.

When you put good seeds in a child, they will grow and develop to bring fruitful life out to fulfil the child's mission and purpose on earth. Engage children with principles and methods that are systematic, not just random approach to work with. Create a desire in them to be independent and responsible. Get them to follow through and complete tasks. Plan work for them in bite-size for the day/week, and make them report back on the challenges they had faced.

Praise specific aspects of the work done. For example, "You cleaned up nicely, Laura. " If the child says, "Did I do it well?" Don't just give a general answer and say yes. At that sort of vague answer, the child will see himself as adequate all round. But that could be a false assumption. If, rather, you comment on a specific part that was good, you give room for improvement. Make children feel important. Give appropriate praise and encouragement for creativity, and the child will be more likely to complete the tasks again in the future.

Allow your teens the opportunity for autonomy and freedom. Just because you brought them into this world, it does not mean you should control every aspect of their life and development. When I talk about freedom, I mean freedom to do the right things, but also to supervise the things they are doing. Notice good qualities and tell them. Don't just notice the wrong things and what they are not doing right. Compliment them for right conducts. Girls in particular who are not used to compliments can often be surprised upon hearing positive things in the outside world.

Write letters to your children from where you are, telling them of their good qualities and what you see in them, not just their look; because, they will pay so much attention to their outer look, thinking that is what makes them, even though their inner values matter more.

Don't punish children after you have suffered a trauma. When upset, angry or tired, listen to children with undivided attention, so that it develops in them to listen to people too. Reading helps create a love for nature and the general world. It also helps with thinking to make decisions and to take responsibility. Train the mind to be inactive consciousness so it is not lost.

Daydreaming kills time. That's when a five minutes job takes five hours. To live in active consciousness, you have to query yourself every five seconds to ensure you maintain focus. Asking realistic questions such as, what am I doing now, or what is the book I am reading saying will re-route your thought. Train your mind to follow the guidelines set out in this book - for your benefit and the benefit of your child.

Children are to take the initiative and think of the consequences of their actions. Say, whether to wear trainers instead of slippers to wash a car. Criticism from parents is to be positive and help the child grow as an individual, not to kill the child's initiative and independence. Allow them the freedom to make their own conscious decisions, unless there is a strong chance it will go badly, but you need to be sure.

Communicating Love By Eye Contact

A teenage girl may say, "Helen's parents treat her better than my parents. " This sort of girl must develop the right mind that she is loved as this flows into any family she will make in future. Hugs, kisses and gentle touches are necessary as they help to protect children's sense of value and love. This way, they feel important in the family and with friends. A lot of boys look for the opposite sex because they have not been hugged or kissed.

Give chores that equal a child's ability. And if not done right the first time, give warning. If not done the second time, give a reminder. If not done the third time, punish; and this helps children develop being responsible and develop habits of hard work. People who take responsibility are generally better, smarter, happier and successful.

Healthy activities, when appropriate and equitably measured, prevent idleness and mischief in children. Those who develop hard work skills don't grow to live off others. Don't kill earlier initiatives in 2-5 years olds. Children who are engaged in physical work do study well. Children not involved in house chores face challenges because they are not used to it. Work is education.

Children must not be afraid of failure or ashamed to ask for help; nor afraid to give fair treatment to people. Relationships break down because of deception. Children must always be encouraged to create an atmosphere of trust.

PLEASE LEAVE A 1-CLICK REVIEW!

Thank you for reading this book and engaging in the next step to establishing positive child development. I hope this book help you in the same way it has helped many others.

I would really appreciate if you could take 60 seconds to write a short review for this book on Amazon, even if it's just a few sentences! Your help in spreading the word is greatly appreciated. Reviews from readers like you make a huge difference in helping new readers find helpful books like this one. I joyfully read every single review.

Just click on the link below and you will be taken straight to the review page on Amazon.

Thank you!

101 Tips
for
Child
Development

Proven Methods for Raising Children and Improving
Kids Behavior with Whole Brain Training

BUKKY EKINE-OGUNLANA

<u>Review Book Here</u>

CONCLUSION

Thank you for buying this book. I hope it has taught you different ways to help your children develop the appropriate skills. Parenting is a noble calling, and bringing up confident, successful and happy children isn't an easy task.

Every parent's dream is to raise successful and happy children. I hope this book has made your duty as a parent less daunting. I also hope the skills set enunciated helps to make your dreams as a parent come true.

I implore you to take one step at a time and take each day as it comes. I believe you can do it. I believe you are up to the challenge. I also believe you'll be successful at it.

This is to your children turning out to be future leaders!

After reading the book in its entirety, please feel free to leave some feedback and share your stories with me.

Thank you.

ABOUT THE BOOK

Every parent wants to instil their core values and beliefs in their children. They make great grand plans and dream big dreams, but when it comes to the actual execution of those lofty ideas, some parents find themselves lost in the fray of nurturing, providing for, chauffeuring children to and fro, and trying to stay on top of the many items on their growing to-do lists.

101 Tips for Child Development is the quintessential guide to teaching your children how to be loving, kind, intelligent, compassionate, and responsibility-ready individuals who will thrive in the world and have no difficulties navigating the sometimes-complicated journeys they may experience.

This guide walks parents through every aspect of teaching life's most essential and necessary skills. Unlike other products on the market, this book looks at where children are in their brain and emotional development and suggests the best practices to help them not only absorb the information but learn how to use it in their everyday lives.

If you're eager to start your child or children on the right path, ***101 Tips for Child Development*** is your ready tool for achieving that goal!

OTHER BOOKS YOU'LL LOVE!

TIPS FOR
#UNIVERSITY
LIFE
BUKKY E KINE-OGUNLANA

DEVELOPING
YOURSELF
AS A
TEENAGER
BUKKY EKINE-OGUNLANA

GUIDE FOR
BOARDING
SCHOOL LIFE
BUKKY EKINE-OGUNLANA

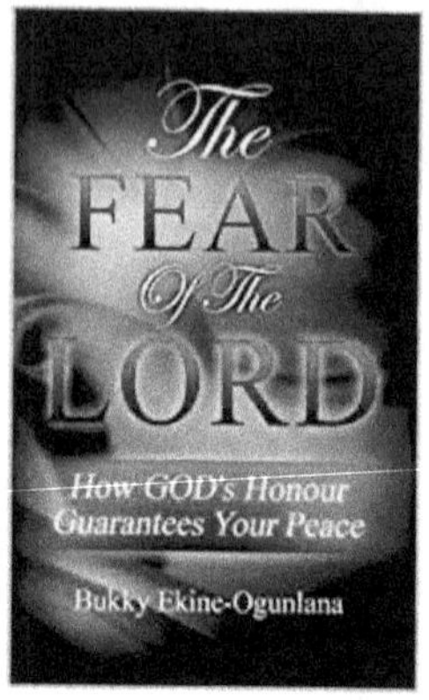

REFERENCES

1. https://cchp.ucsf.edu/sites/g/files/tkssra181/f/
   SelfEsteem_en0710.pdf

2. https://www.theseus.fi/bitstream/handle/10024/
   50239/Anttila_Marianna_Saikkonen_Pinja.pdf

3. https://ijcat.com/archives/volume5/issue2/
   ijcatr05021006.pdf

4. https://www.harvey.k-state.edu/family-and-consumer-
   sciences/family_and_child_development/
   documents/CommunicatingwTeenTrust.pdf

5. https://www.researchgate.net/
   publication/283721084_Early_Reading_Development

6. https://www.understood.org/en/friends-feelings/
   empowering-your-child/building-on-strengths/
   download-hands-on-activity-to-identify-your-child-
   strengths

7. https://www.wfm.noaa.gov/pdfs/
   ParentingYourTeen_Handout1.pdf

8. https://www.helpguide.org/articles/depression/parents-guide-to-teen-depression.htm?pdf=13027

9. https://www2.ed.gov/parents/academic/help/adolescence/adolescence.pdf

10. http://centerforchildwelfare.org/kb/prprouthome/Helping%20Your%20Children%20Navigate%20Their%20Teenage%20Years.pdf

11. https://www.childrensmn.org/images/family_resource_pdf/027121.pdf

12. https://educationnorthwest.org/sites/default/files/developing-empathy-in-children-and-youth.pdf

13. http://drkateaubrey.com/wp-content/uploads/2016/02/Parenting-Your-Strong-Willed-Child.pdf

14. https://www.researchgate.net/publication/263227023_Family_Time_Activities_and_Adolescents

15. https://parenting-ed.org/wp-content/themes/parenting-ed/files/handouts/communication-parent-to-child.pdf

16. https://www.wikihow.mom/Trust-Your-Teenager

17. https://www.statmodel.com/download/Meeus,%20vd%20Schoot,%20Klimstra%20&.pdf

18. https://www.nap.edu/resource/19401/ProfKnowCompFINAL.pdf

19. http://www.delmarlearning.com/companions/content/1418019224/AdditionalSupport/box11.1.pdf

20. http://resources.beyondblue.org.au/prism/file?token=BL/1810_A

21. https://exeter.anglican.org/wp-content/uploads/2014/11/Listening-to-children-leaflet_NCB.pdf

22. https://www.researchgate.net/

publication/312600262_Creative_Thinking_among_Presc
hool_Children

23. https://www.gutenberg.org/files/15114/15114-pdf.pdf

24. https://discovery.ucl.ac.uk/id/eprint/1522668/1/Thesis%
20Moulton%20V%20281016.pdf

25. https://www.bda.uk.com/
foodfacts/healthyeatingchildren.pdf

26. http://www.tuskmont.org/uploads/1/7/7/2/
17728377/follow_the_child_trust_the_child.pdf

27. https://www.apa.org/pi/families/resources/develop.pdf

28. https://extension.colostate.edu/docs/pubs/
consumer/10249.pdf

29. https://www.empoweringparents.com/article/risky-teen-
behavior-can-you-trust-your-child-again/

30. http://www.wecf.eu/download/2018/05%20May/
WSSPPublicationENPartC-MHMchapter.pdf

101 TIPS FOR HELPING WITH YOUR CHILD'S LEARNING

PROVEN STRATEGIES FOR ACCELERATED LEARNING AND RAISING SMART CHILDREN USING POSITIVE PARENTING SKILLS

This book is dedicated to our three amazing children (Peace, Joshua and Caleb) and all the beautiful children all over the world who over the years have passed through the T.C.E.C 6-16 years program. Thanks for the opportunity to serve you and invest in your colourful and bright future.

INTRODUCTION

Studies have shown that children are more active and successful in school when parents are interested in their learning and homework [1]. Many resources in books and on the internet will show you that throughout your child's education, a robust family framework that is able to support them is significantly beneficial in how they process new information and further develop their knowledge of critical areas. Of course, helping your children with learning or their homework doesn't require you to spend several hours behind a desk. As a parent, you can develop your child's learning by improving reading and spelling abilities in your child, teaching your child mathematics or English language at home, demonstrating organisation and study skills, or explaining a difficult problem. Improving your child's behaviour at school, giving them the chance to achieve higher grades are some of the benefits you start to gain when you involve yourself with your child's learning [2]. What if getting involved in your child's learning could help to reduce his/her behavioural problems at school, improve his/her grades or help him/her enjoy school the more? Getting involved in your child's learning doesn't demand that you have an educational background or a big fat account. Your involvement in your child's learning will further make him successful at home. Homework time gives you an insight into your child's life at school, giving you the opportunity to see what their day has been about [3].

In addition to improving your child's grade at school, getting involved in your child's learning helps to improve your child's behaviour and social skills at school. Studies have shown that children who are guided by their parents are less likely to be suspended, less likely to skip school, less likely to disrupt the class and less likely to fail a subject.

Children that are supported both at home and school have more self-confidence, they develop positive attitudes about school, and they place much priority on academic achievement. Children do not only benefit when parents are involved in their learning. No, parents also benefits! When parents are involved in their kid's education, they are more confident in their parenting skills, and there's a high possibility for them to continue their education.

This book "101 tips for helping with your child's learning" is written for parents to get involved in their child's education and learning. This book is as a result of my experience as a teacher at the tuition centre; we have a tuition centre where we help children with Mathematics, English, reading and spelling tuition. This book will show the secrets and tactics of teaching to help parents get involved in their children's education. This paperback is divided into five chapters, and each section addresses the tactics and secrets that are required for parents to get involved in their child's learning. Each chapter sums up 101 ways to help develop your child's learning.

Please get in touch and provide us with your honest, unfiltered feedback/review on how useful this book was to you. It will be much appreciated and helpful to hear as many opinions and responses to this book as possible.

1

DEVELOPING READING SKILLS

DEVELOPING READING SKILLS IN CHILDREN

As a teacher, teaching students how to read is one of my passions. In my experience, I found that most children do not start reading until around 4-6 years old. However, the strategies listed in this chapter are helpful for children of all ages. Do not practice these strategies at a go and do not pressurize your child to practice all the strategies immediately. At the tuition centre, we have met with parents who come to ask how they can help their children learn to read at home. This is not a surprise because reading is an essential skill that every child is expected to learn. Reading plays a critical role in the success of a child at school. Teaching children how to read is a process, and the information detailed in this chapter is for you to carry out or practice when your child is ready. I should also mention that although the strategies listed below are labelled as steps, they are not in consecutive order or in the order of importance.

Here are some practical ways by which parents can help their young child or teen learn how to read.

Teaching children how to read

Parents are often told that teaching children how to read at the early years is unwholesome, but this is not entirely true. In fact, the effect of doing so is different in every case, for some it can bring on unnecessary anxiety, but for others it is an opportunity to excel and thrive. Introducing children to engage with and develop literacy skills in their early years isn't harmful, most of the time. I started reading to my children the day I gave birth to them. Studies have shown that the inner ear of a foetus during pregnancy fully develops at 20 weeks. This indicates that your baby is ready to listen and learn from the first day of delivery. As babies grow, they use their hearing to process information about the world around them [4]. Though, the "implications of early teaching" has been studied and discussed for several years; there hasn't been a piece of single evidence to convince readers that reading to children at the early years is harmful. On the flip side, there are several hundreds of studies that show the benefits of reading to children in their early years. When you are reading to your child, you are teaching the child to listen.The child might be looking at your face or not make any move or he might not respond but the child is listening ,when children learn to listen properly, they will learn to decode information accurately.

Why children fail in comprehension is because they have not been well thought on how to listen and interpret what they have read. This must be taught deliberately at home.

Listening is learnt at home and school only takes advantage of it. Teachers assume that children have been taught how to listen from home.

1. Teaching literacy is similar to teaching other essential skills

As a parent, you do not need to get a doctorate to raise healthy, happy and smart children. Parents have been in the business of teaching their children how to read since the dawn of time, or at least when the first book was written. Teaching literacy to children is in no way groundbreaking and we're not about to re-invent the wheel in what we tell you. However, the information is certainly something you need to know, and often a lot of this information isn't passed through generations, though it should be. Our parents successfully taught us how to eat with a fork or spoon, how to keep fingers away from the nose, how to use a potty and how to say "sorry," "please" and "thank you." These basic and essential skills can either be taught to children pleasantly or as a painful chore, that is skills can also be taught unpleasantly by punishing or yelling. As with all other essential skills, reading can also be taught to children. If you show your 16-month-old child a book and he doesn't show interest, put the book away and try again later. But definitely don't accept defeat. Perseverance is critical in this situation, and though it may not be the right time right now, next time your child may just show interest. Similarly, If your child doesn't get how to write correctly the first time and ends up writing in a backward manner, don't fret. Enjoy the journey with your child. Appreciate that we all learn in different ways, at different speeds - no matter what the subject or the time in your life. Remember, we're all born ready and eager to learn [5].

2. Talk to your children a lot

There's no harm in talking to your child from her early years. Talk to her, sing to her/him about anything, talk about her/his nose, mouth, ears, fingers, and eyes. Talk to her about her/his family, dad, mom, and older siblings. You can also talk to her/him when she/he sleeps, eats, burp or yawn. Some parents tend to think that talking to a child when she's still a baby is crazy because a baby doesn't understand yet. I beg to differ; reading is a language activity and as such, to learn the language, you need to hear it before you can speak it. As a matter of fact, studies have shown that teaching by way of saying a variety of words to your young child or baby helps in the development of literacy skills. I suppose the phrase "catch them when they are young" also applies to reading. Not only that, but communicating is also done via social cues, tone of voice and body language - things that babies, infants and children are very responsive to. So, talking as well as using your body language to communicate is an effective way of spurring on their development. Many studies go one step further, suggesting the use of a silly voice is beneficial in your child picking up language [6].

3. Read to your child

I describe reading to children as the foundation of developing a solid reading skill. Reading to children is a good idea, and it helps. There are several alternatives to reading for parents who can't read English; such parents could use an audiobook but for parents who can read English, reading a story or a book to a child is an excellent idea as it helps to improve literacy skills in children. Several studies have confirmed that reading to children helps to improve their literacy skills. When you read to a child, you expose them to vocabulary that is richer than the spoken words they hear from adults who talk to them. This has a positive impact on their intelligence, language and literacy achievement as they grow. There are quite a number of beautiful books to read to children; you can visit your local library to choose from the vast array of adventure books to read to children.

Truth be told, the process of teaching your child how to read is one that starts at infancy though I do not advise that you teach your baby reading with flashcards. No. I am encouraging you to start reading with your baby a day after you welcome her into your home. Besides the fact that the time is a special bonding time for mothers and babies, it's also a perfect time to instil love for books. You need to teach your child not just to read, but to enjoy reading. Failure to teach your child to enjoy reading from an early age will most likely frustrate their efforts to enjoy reading down the road. There's no limit to the books to read to your child in a day, the number of books you read is entirely up to you. You can read at least 3-4 books a day while your child is young but as she gets older, make it a habit to read together for at least 30 minutes daily.

One study in particular details how parents play a vital role in the development of cognitive and reading skills by reading to their children from a young age. Giving us an insight that when we frequently read to children around the ages of 4 and 5, it has a significant positive effect on them all the way up to around the age of 10 or 11 [7].

Here are suggestions of books to read to your child. These are just suggestions; you can always read whatever your child enjoys.

- Birth - One year: Songbooks, Bible stories, Psalms, Lullabies, Cloth books (with different textures), Board Books (with pictures).
- One year – Three years: Songbooks, Bible stories, Psalms, Rhyming Books, Short-Story board books.
- Three years - Five Years: Song Books, Bible stories Psalms, Alphabet Books, Rhyming books and Picture Books.

4. Have your child tell you a story

Another great way to introduce children to reading is to listen to their story or take their dictation. Have them make up a story or recount their experience. Their story maybe something like, "I like grandma," "I like Chicken," "I like my brother." Write the stories as they are being told and then read aloud. While reading, make sure to point at the words as you read them or point at the words when your child is reading them. Over time, your child would be able to identify words such as "like" or "I" even without pointing at them.

Not only is this good for literacy development and communication, it also encourages creativity - when a child is crafting their own story, they are utilising their imagination and allowing it to reach new heights. In the process, they are learning a love for language and building their confidence [8].

5. Teach your child phonemic awareness.

Your young child doesn't have the ability to hear the sounds within words. She hears "dog," but she doesn't hear the sound or phonemes duh - aw- guh). To make your child a reader, you need to teach them how to learn the sounds or phonemes in words. For example, say a word and then break it down into phonemes; chair - ch-ch-ch-air. "Phonemes," which are composed of short vowels, consonants, digraphs, and long vowels are the smallest sounds in the English Language. Phonemic awareness entails learning sounds and how to manage them within a word. Digraphs are unique sounds that are made up of single letters such as sh, th, ch, etc. Phonics involves learning how to spell sounds as well as the rules that bind the English language. Though phonics is an essential component of spelling and reading, it shouldn't be made the main focus. Teaching your kid the rules of phonics will help her learn to decode and spell. At the tuition centre, we use the Pathways to Reading program as our phonics and phonemic awareness, and it sure makes learning all of the complicated spellings fun. However, we do not advise that parents use it until children are in kindergarten, first grade or year 1, that is ages 5-7.

6. Teach phonics (letter names and their sounds).

To write words or sound out words, there is a need for your child to know the letter sounds. Young children learn letter sounds in kindergarten, and parents can also teach them. All you will need is a paper and pencil, but you can also get ABC books, cards, charts, floor mats, magnet letters, and puzzles. Keep the lessons fun and brief; the lesson should be no more than 10 minutes for young children as children tend to attend to activities that interest them for 10-15 minutes without getting distracted.

7. **Listen to your child read**

Have your child read to you. When she starts bringing books home, have her read them to you. If she doesn't sound clear or reasonable at the first read, have her read the book all over again. You can guide her by reading the book to her first before she reads it herself. Studies have shown that doing this repeatedly helps the kids to become better readers both at home and school.

Additionally, you can structure this activity and give it the foundations to provide a robust learning framework for your child. Go through the process of allowing your child to select a book and explain the reason they chose the book. The next step of action would be to encourage them to read the book and afterwards ask them what was happening, this way you can learn of their comprehension skills. After the reading session is complete, you can have a more in-depth discussion on what the book was about and how the characters were feeling. This ensures that your child is getting the most from every opportunity they have to read [9].

8. **Promote writing**

While you are teaching your child how to read, make sure to promote writing. Literacy involves writing and reading so have magazines and books available for your children. Also, it's helpful to have crayons, pencils, papers, and markers available for your child to learn how to write. You can encourage your child to write by writing short letters or notes to her. Before you know it, she will start writing letters or notes back to you.

9. **Ask questions**

When your child reads to you, have her retell the information or story. When your child reads a story, ask her questions. You can ask her who and what the story is about and if she shares information with you, ask her what the information is about and how it works.

Reading isn't just about sounding out words; it involves thinking about the story or text and remembering the events and ideas. Do not just read to your child, ask questions. Besides encouraging your child to relate with the book being read, asking your child questions while reading to her also helps to develop her ability to fully grasp what you are reading. Your main objective when reading to your child should not just be to get your child to sound out words. Your objective should be helping your child grasp what's being read. You'd be surprised that children who can sound words and read with high fluency might find it difficult to fully grasp what they are reading. What's the point of reading when a child cannot grasp what he is reading? Ask your kid questions to be sure that she comprehends what's being read. When your child is still young, ask her questions such as, "Do you see the dog?" while pointing to the picture of the dog. Asking questions will not only improve her vocabulary, but it will also encourage interaction with the book she's reading. Once your child is around 2-3 years, ask her questions before, while reading the book and after reading the book. Show her the cover of the book before reading and ask her to predict what the book is about. While reading the book, ask her why she thinks a particular character made a choice. In a case where a character is portraying a strong emotion, identify the emotion and ask her if she has ever felt the emotion. After reading the book, ask her what happened in the book or what she learnt from the book.

10. Make reading a regular activity at your home.

Make reading a regular activity at your home, and your children will thank you for it. I recollected when I was 9 years old, my mom would make me read for 30 minutes after lunch. We went to the book collection to get books to start my new activity, and this regular activity of mine made me a lifelong reader. Set aside time for everyone to read a book with no distractions. Do not just make the time a reading time, make the time fun and enjoyable.

11. Be a good example (good reader)

Even if your child develops an interest in reading from an early age, her interest will quickly reduce if she doesn't see reading being practised in her home. Even if you are not an enthusiastic reader, make sure that your child sees you reading for a few minutes. You can read a cookbook, bible, novel or a magazine, whatever rocks your boat. The point is to show your child that everyone reads, adults inclusive. As parents, we get wrapped up with the things our children should do to be successful forgetting that children learn by example.

Various studies suggest that children will mimic the behaviours and attitudes of their parents, so it's always best to go into everything educational with an open mind, as not to deter them from participating in developing skills in that area. It can be argued that children are more likely to succeed and more easily develop their skillset when their parents have succeeded in their educational journeys too [10].

12. Identify letters in natural settings

As children approach a certain age, parents tend to force them to learn the name of letters. We buy DVDs or flashcards in a bid to teach our children the name of the letters. Then we go-ahead to drill our young child over and over just for them to learn letters. Don't do this, leave your child to be a child and grab the teachable moments as they come. The mind of children are like sponges capable of learning alphabets from drilling, but drilling isn't an effective method of teaching that produces long-term results. As your child grows, she will be curious about the letters she sees around, and she will ask questions. That's not the time to drill your child but the time to use practical applications to teach your child. I am not saying that teaching your child alphabets isn't essential, but what's more important is how you teach her. Have in mind that the ultimate goal when teaching your child how to read or write is to raise a lifelong reader who's passionate about reading and not just a child who memorized letters without any significance.

13. Include multiple domains of development

I have found that children learn what they are being taught when different areas of development or different senses are incorporated. This is why hands-on teaching is more applicable and retained by children. The moment your child shows interest in letters, you should start using natural settings to identify the letters and also implement activities that include as many senses as possible. When it comes to developing letter recognition and reading skills in children, there are a number of ways to include multiple domains of development. Through the process of cutting, glueing and creating alphabet crafts to teach your child the shape of a letter as well as the sound of the letter. Games that involve gross motor skills is an excellent way of incorporating movement. Every child loves singing and rhyming so, identify the strengths and interests of your child and incorporate activities that fit them.

If you are stuck for specific ideas then inspiration for such activities can be found by a quick search on the internet. Luckily, there are thousands of resources that can help you, many of which are very useful.

14. Classify the genre

Children around 5 years can identify the difference between reality and make-belief. I advise that you teach your child the different genres of the book while you are reading together. Though teaching your child, the different genres of the book seem like a complicated or difficult task; it's not entirely difficult. I have listed five genres of books to teach your little one. You can use "type" in the place of "genre" if the type is easier to remember.

- Nonfiction books - Real facts or stories about people, places or animals.
- Fantasy - Not real. Things or events that cannot happen in real life. Talking animals or magical events.
- Realistic fiction - A made-up story that can happen in real life since the situations and characters are believable.
- Song Books
- Alphabet Books

To classify a book into a specific type or genre, your child needs to summarize the book and remember the details of the book. Then, he has to use the book information to decide the type of genre the book falls under. While doing this, your child will be remembering the details of similar books in the same genre and thereby making connections between the books. Though this activity may take time, it's sure to pack a punch of processing and thought in your child's brain. You should know that there are some books like phonics readers which do not fall under any of the listed genres. I would advise that you carry out this exercise using quality children's literature, such books can be found in libraries. Have in mind that the ultimate goal for this exercise is to help your child understand what he's reading. When you reinforce your child to reflect on and remember the details of the book he read, you are modelling him to do what you hope he'll do independently in the nearest future.

In the research process for this book, we found one method for teaching children the difference between non-fiction and fiction was repeatedly cropping up. This method was the poster method; providing children with posters with a short definition of each of the terms, alongside related imagery. For non-fiction, the images were all from the real world, however with the fiction poster the pictures were of cartoon-like characters or mythical animals. Further defining what is real as non-fiction and what is a fantasy as fiction [11].

15. Word Families

Simply put, word families are words that sound identically. Teaching children word families helps them identify the pattern in reading. Identifying the pattern in reading is vital as it helps children to start reading by grouping the sets of letters in a word. The first set of letters in a word is referred to as the onset while the last part is called the rime. Though there are changes to onset, work families share a similar rhyme. For instance, once your child has identified the word "pop," he will find it easy to read other words with similar rime such as hop, cop, stop, mop or top.

16. Decoding

Decoding is often described as "sounding it out." Though decoding is an element to consider when teaching your child how to read, it's not the essential element. Once your child can identify the sounds of each letter, she is ready to put words together. For instance, when you are teaching your child to pronounce short words such as cat, encourage her to pronounce individual sound /c/, /a/, /t/ before putting them together as "cat." As your child learns how to decode words with accuracy and more frequency, she will be proficient at identifying words automatically. This exercise is a tedious one, so there's a need for you to incorporate things that will make it fun.

Though we state this isn't one of the essential elements in teaching your child to read, there are sources on the internet and in academic journals that do stake significant importance on this activity in their early development of children. "Early attainment of decoding skill is essential because this early skill accurately predicts later skill in reading comprehension. There is persuasive and strong evidence that children who get off to a slow start rarely become strong readers.

Early learning of the code leads to wider reading habits both in and out of school" [12].

17. Sight words

Sight words which are otherwise known as high-frequency words are common words in the English language that don't follow the rules of phonics. Thus they are difficult to sound phonetically. You have to teach your child to memorize sight words. Sight words need to be memorized for your child to become an accurate and precise reader. You do not have to start with a long list of sight words. Start teaching your child a few words at a time. Activities such as Sight Word Bingo makes learning and memorizing sight words a fun activity.

As you must have probably noticed, teaching your child how to read doesn't have a specific formula. The tips and strategies listed in this chapter are simple but effective, and they are not meant to be used as a checklist. Do not use these strategies as a checklist and think that once you have implemented all these strategies, your child will be proficient at reading. This chapter provides information to use as a guide while creating a learning environment that will foster the growth of your kid as a reader. Don't be in a rush and do not over-stretch your child. While it's critical to take advantage of the early years learning time, it's more important to allow your child to be a child.

Here are some practical tips for implementing every day; these tips are a summary of the strategies discussed in this chapter. Note that all the strategies discussed in this chapter cannot be implemented on all ages, so use your discretion to determine the strategy that is best for your child.

- Develop a habit of reading to your child every day.
- Make sure you ask your child questions before, while reading and after reading.

- Be a good example, that is be a good reader yourself.
- When teaching your child letters and sounds, include as many senses as possible.
- Read different varieties of book and ask your child to guess the genre.
- Make rhyming a fun activity.
- Teach your child to pronounce short words.
- Practice memorizing sight words every day and most importantly, have fun reading together with your child.

2

HOW TO IMPROVE THE SPELLING ABILITIES OF YOUR CHILD

The role of a mother or father in helping children to read, write and spell is vital. No doubt, children who are good spellers are better readers.

Here are some fun and helpful ways to improve your child's spelling.

18. Play the spelling word memory game

Create two sets of word cards and play the spelling word memory game by spreading the cards so they face down and then take turns to flip two cards at once to find a pair. Though it may not seem particularly challenging, it means that the children are being exposed to a repeated set list of words. This way, the point is being hammered home of what those particular words look like, how to decode them and how to spell them. It's also an entertaining game for children where they can learn outside of the traditional classroom environment and experience.

19. Play the flip four steps game

This game allows your child to practice reading, spelling and writing down words. Have your child turn over a word card, identify the word, pronounce the word, say the letters, turn the card over and write down the word on a paper.

20. Read, read, read

The more the kids read, the more they will start memorizing the spelling of words. Keep in mind that picture books contain more simple words than early reader books, so do not replace picture books with more educational books. Instead you should move onto more educational/further developed reading materials only when your child is ready to do so.

Expanding on their knowledge, tastes and vocabulary skills is crucial to ensuring your child becomes a keen reader, effective communicator and continues to improve their concentration levels [13].

21. Practice spelling

Make spelling practise a regular activity. Keep in mind that spelling isn't an activity you teach a child once and then move on to do something else. Spelling requires review and regular practice.

22. Carry out projects that involve words

Get busy with projects that involve words. Make word collages where you cut words from a book or magazine, attach them to a paper with glue and then write down filler words to form a story.

23. Play word games

Boggle, hangman and scrabble are fun and excellent games for improving spelling. Playing a word game with your child is an easy and exciting way to learn complicated words quickly.

24. Spell and eat

While preparing breakfast, brunch, or lunch, have your child spell a word and reward her with a treat when the word is correctly spelt.

25. Surround your child with printed cards

Label the cupboard and desk of your child with printed cards showing different words to make it easy for her to learn the words every day.

26. Consider Rewarding, not punishment

Ensure to reward your child with stickers, praise, points, treats, and the like. Using positive reinforcement motivates your child to memorize more words than punishing your child when a word is wrongly spelt.

You need to understand that teaching your child to spell words at home requires patience and also demands a non-school setting. Do not try to be a teacher or a parent who commands, instead be a parent who teaches. Keep the spelling activities fun, short and do them regularly.

27. Trace, copy and recall

Fold three columns on a paper and label the first column "trace," label the second column "copy," and the third column "recall". Write the word in the first column labelled trace and have your child trace the letters. Have her copy the word to the second column and finally, hide the first two columns and have her remember the spelling of the word and write it down without guidance.

Fun and exciting spelling games using a pen, pencil, marker and paper

28. Spelling Word Race

Form two teams and have each team take a turn holding the pen. Prepare a list of words and call out a word for the players on the team to write down the word quickly.

Not only does this make things more exciting and fun for your child, it also adds a competitive element to something which may have previously seemed like a relatively dull task.

29. Spelling Puzzle

Create a homemade puzzle by writing words in large letters on an index card. Have your kid cut out each word and then try to put the puzzle back together.

30. Stair steps

Write down words and arrange them like they are stairs, adding a letter one after the other.

- *S*
- *St*
- *Sta*
- *Stai*
- *Stair*

31. Tic-Tac-Toe

Create a large-sized board and play tic-tac-toe. Have each player write down a spelling word. Also, this game can be played in a different way. Have each player use an 'O' or 'X', but to place a mark on the board, each player is required to spell a word correctly.

32. Window Writing

Use unique window safe crayons. Window writing makes learning word spelling fun and exciting. Window safe crayons can be found from various outlets on the high street and retailers on the internet. They are relatively affordable and are great for helping your little one on his/her literacy journey.

33. Flip and Rainbow Write

Flip a word card over and have the child write and paint each flipped word in rainbow colours. The first word should be coloured red, the second-word orange and the third word should be coloured yellow.

34. Water Paint

Using water and a paintbrush, have your child identify words and paint spelling words.

Fun and exciting ways to learn word spelling using a computer and other fun electronics

35. Type it out

Open a word document on a computer. Call spelling words loudly and have your child type the words on the screen. Enlarge the font of the text and make it a cool colour.

36. Spell on Tape

Set the voice recorder on the computer or on your phone and have your child spell words correctly.

37. Video Record

Make a video of your child spelling words. Have her dress up, wear a silly hat or use a silly prop to make the activity more exciting.

38. Karaoke

That karaoke machine can be used as a fun spelling machine. Simply turn it on and have your child spell his words into it.

Though it's not your traditional night of karaoke, it does give your child the spotlight, making them feel louder and more noticeable than before. This is therefore a definite confidence booster.

39. Use Puzzlemaker

Let your child type in all her spelling words and then search for them with the puzzle maker.

40. Use Let them sing it

Let Them Sing It is a site that turns spelling words into a song. Have your child spell words on this site and the word is sung back to your child.

41. Use Spelling City

Spelling City is a site which allows your child to type in his spelling words, learn the words, play games with the words and then take a test.

Fun and exciting ways to learn word spelling using space to run, jump, and play:

42. Chalkboard Race

Form two teams and have a player from each team hold a piece of chalk and stand at a spot away from the chalkboard. Call out a word and have the players run to the board to write the correct spelling. The player who writes the correct spelling first is the winner.

43. Ball Toss

Children form a circle with a ball or with a safe object to pass around. Call out a word then pass the ball to a child, and the child spells the word. If the word is misspelt, the child passes the ball to the next person to spell the word. If the child correctly spells the word, he passes the ball to the next child and the teacher or parent calls out a new word to spell.

44. Swing and Spell

The parent or teacher calls out a word for a child to spell and he spells the word with each back and forth manoeuvres of the swing.

45. Run the Bases

The game starts with the child at a home plate. The parent or teacher calls out a word to spell and the child moves around the base starting with hitting the ball, running from the first base to the second and third base and back to the home plate while spelling the word.

Fun and exciting ways to learn word spelling with anything and everything else

46. Spelling Word Hunt

Have your child circle or highlight the spelling words listed at the back of a newspaper, in a book, text or a magazine.

47. Crazy Words:

Pour body cream, rice or sand on a cookie sheet and have your child write spelling words on the tray with his fingers.

48. Paint bag Writing

Pour poster paint in a gallon-sized Ziploc bag and close it tightly. Have your child write the letters of each word on the paint bag with her fingertips.

49. Stamp It

With the aid of an alphabet letter stamp, have your child stamp spelling words by first looking at the words and writing them with no guidance.

Fun and exciting games to learn word spelling with magnetic letters or letter cards:

50. Word Scramble

Rearrange the letters of each word and have your child arrange them in the right order. Make sure to point out families and patterns.

51. Word Train

Have your child form a word train by forming a new word with the last letter of the first word. For example, tap - pan - net.

52. Examine the Word

Pick a spelling word, look at the word closely and talk to your child about the tough parts of the word. Teach your child silly ways to remember the tough parts of a spelling word. For example, 'chocolate' has an 'o' in the middle because chocolate is sweet.

Creativity

Probably the most crucial aspect in a child's educational journey to literacy competence and success is opening their mind to new ideas, innovative thinking and breaking the mould. When your child first begins to read, there will be many new ideas presented to them. Whether it's a talking dog - something we would consider very out of the ordinary as it is entirely unrealistic, or whether it's an astronaut going to space - something very realistic but bizarre to somebody who doesn't know anything outside of their own home, school and town.

Embracing your child's creativity, encouraging them to think in the same way as the writers whose pieces of fiction they are reading can be hugely beneficial. As we have already mentioned, you should be encouraging your child to tell stories and get their brain working creatively, but also open their mind up to as many new situations as possible. Ensure they know astronauts are real, ensure they know dogs can't really talk - but most importantly, ensure they know that anything can happen in a book and that the world is their oyster. Make it fun, keep it educational and keep their attention in the process.

You can achieve this through first educating them on it, then by inviting them to tell you a bedtime story, or write something new.

A friend once told me that she encouraged her son to write her a story and what she read was incredible. It was a blend of characters he had seen on television, they joined forces and went on to stop a bad guy who had a very evil plan. Though his characters weren't anything new, there was a clear narrative, fantastical elements and the themes were heavily focused on friendship and teamwork. It was clear that her child had effectively utilised his literacy skills to form his own story. He was combining theory with practicality and forming new ideas that would have stayed dormant in his mind otherwise.

3

SIMPLE STRATEGIES FOR TEACHING YOUR CHILD MATHEMATICS AT HOME

Teaching your child mathematics at home is as easy as adding 1+1 = 2. There are a number of methods to teach your child mathematics at home without having a pencil and paper. It's essential for your child to understand mathematics. Good knowledge of math is needed to get your child through her study years. Math is applicable both outside and inside the school. Truth be told, math can be somewhat dull and challenging for kids, but with a little teaching at home, maths can quickly become an exciting subject. You can help make mathematics an intriguing subject for your child by taking away the seriousness of math and turning the subject into a fun and creative activity.

Particularly when your children reaches the age of 11 all the way up to the age of 16, you'll likely notice that they seem disengaged with learning. This is as a result of the sheer number of distractions in their social lives between those ages. Between their social lives and wanting to get invited to all the outings, they don't really have much time or attention for learning - and even when they are doing it, their minds are often elsewhere. Whether it's English or Mathematics, children between the ages of 11 and 16 probably find their teachers boring, the subjects dull and in the case of Mathematics, it can seem difficult to see how relevant the subject will be in later life.

Particularly in the case of algebra, it's so easy for a child between the ages of 11 and 16 to completely disregard the topic as irrelevant, pointless and ultimately, a waste of time. So, it's essential to engage your child in Mathematics based activities at home too, probably more-so than literacy-based activities.

This chapter discusses the quick and easy strategies to teach children mathematics at home and turn them into young mathematicians.

53. Begin with counting

When it comes to mathematics, numbers are significant. Teaching mathematics starts with your child identifying her numbers. You can teach your kid how to count with the same strategies you will employ to teach her mathematics. You can have her memorize numbers as you call them or have her pick up numbers by counting objects from 1-10. You need to understand that the method that works for one child may work or not work for the other child. Once your child has learnt how to count, you can start teaching her some simple math principles and before you know it, she will be subtracting and adding.

54. Use Everyday Objects

You have everything needed to teach your child mathematics at home. You have enough objects at your disposal; pennies, buttons, cars, books, money, soup cans, fruits, and trees. Mathematics is easy to teach a child when you have physical objects at your disposal to count, subtract, add and multiply. Everyday objects also teach children that objects need not be identical before they can be used in mathematics. Teaching your child to count mangoes is a great lesson but you'd agree with me that counting oranges, apples, watermelons and mangoes helps to expand his thought process. He's counting various objects instead of counting routine numbers 1-10.

55. Play Math Games

There are games in the market to help teach your child mathematics. For example, adding dice and Hi Ho Cherry-O teaches simple addition while Ladders and Chutes will introduce your child to numbers 1-100. Classic games such as Monopoly, Life, PayDay and Yahtzee are excellent tools for addition and subtraction. You can also create a math game from your imagination. Have your child play a math scavenger hunt. Write a number on the driveway with chalk, ask your child fundamental math question and have him answer by running to the correct number on the driveway. Whatever the math game you choose, make sure the game will make your child enjoy mathematics rather than see mathematics as an educational drill.

56. Bake Cookies

A soft cookie is an excellent resource for teaching mathematics. While your child can count cookies, you can also teach your child fractions using a fresh batch of cookies. Teach your kids how to cut a cookie into halves, fourths or eighths with a plastic knife. Making fractions from a whole visually leaves an impression in your child's mind. Use small cookie pieces to teach your child how to add and subtract fraction. For instance, with small cookie pieces, show your child that two halves of a small cookie make a whole cookie (1/2 of a cookie + 1/2 of a cookie = 1 whole cookie). You also can make your playdough or use raw cookie dough as an alternative to baking cookies. Your child cannot eat raw cookie fractions after learning maths, but you can keep the cookie dough to reuse for the math lesson.

57. Invest in Abacus or traditional tools

You do not need to download a fancy app on your laptop to teach your child mathematics at home. Instead, use traditional math toys like an abacus. An abacus helps to teach children math skills starting from counting to addition and subtraction. An abacus is reliable as it doesn't run down on battery power or break like a toy laptop.

An abacus is a useful and excellent resource for teaching kids' addition, multiplication, subtraction and division. Even the smallest hands enjoy playing with an abacus. Besides teaching your child basic subtraction, addition, multiplication or division, an abacus also helps to develop problem-solving skills in children.

58. Test Flash Cards

Though flashcards can show the addition of two numbers, letting children do the counting themselves work better. Take a step further by evaluating the learning preferences of your child by trying both manual counting and flash cards. While some children learn mathematics better by counting pictures on a card, others learn by seeing the answer to a sum on a card. Others will not get the concept fully until they count physical objects. Try out different methods to be sure of the method that works best for your child.

59. Make Math a Daily Activity

Incorporate mathematics into the daily routine of your child. Help your child benefit from math lesson by incorporating it in his daily life and at the same time, make sure to set goals that they can achieve in a lesson.

60. Show your child that mathematics is fun

Ask your child basic and simple mathematics questions in a fun and exciting way.

Ask questions such as:

- How many black cars do you see at a red light?
- How many boxes of crackers can we buy with £10 at the grocery store?
- When you go to the doctor's office, ask your child the

number of the kids that will be left in the waiting room after three kids have been attended to.

- While having lunch, ask your child the amount of food you would have left if you only ate 1/4 of the food.
- While driving on the freeway, ask your child to add up the numbers on the license plate of the vehicle driving in front of your car.
- Ask your child how much diapers cost if there's a discount of 25%.
- How many trousers are you putting into the washing machine?
- If you are asked to share eight quarters between four people, how many quarters would you give each person?

Once you show your child that math can be fun and exciting, she will be passionate about learning mathematics. Once your child is passionate about learning, there's no stopping for him.

61. Number everything

Start numbering everything right from the early years of your child. Count his fingers and toes while changing his diaper. Count the segments of mandarin you give him, count the oranges you place in a bag at the grocery store. The idea is to take advantage of any opportunity that allows your child to count. When you start teaching your child how to count from his early years, you can be rest assured that he will know his numbers by the time he's ready for pre-school.

62. The TV can be educational

If you do not allow your children to watch TV programs, break the rule and allow them to watch Sesame Street. Sesame Street is a children TV series that teaches children cognitive skills, including mathematics. Mickey Mouse Clubhouse and Numbers around the Globe are both TV programs that teach young children how to count.

63. Make math a game

Learning is always fun when it's made into a game. Here are a few fun games to help teach your child math at home.

Set the table

Have your child set the table for a specific amount of people with unbreakable crockery and cutlery. As he sets the cups and plates, count the numbers loudly and encourage him to repeat after you.

64. Size comparison

Instruct your child to arrange his toy dinosaurs or toy cars from the smallest to the biggest. Pick two toys of different sizes and ask him to identify the smaller and bigger size.

65. Patterns

Lego and other blocks are a great resource to form patterns with. You can also form patterns with shape or colour.

66. Incorporate the lingo

Make sure to incorporate math concept words when discussing everyday things with your child. Use words such as "a few", "a lot," or "some". The words won't be new or strange to him when he has to use the words in the classroom.

67. Shapes

Introduce your child to shapes by identifying or naming the shapes you see in the garden or in the house.

68. Junior Monopoly

While junior monopoly is appropriate for older kids, it can be used to teach children math skills through the paper cash and it can also serve as a way of bonding the family.

69. Piggybank

A piggy bank is an excellent way to teach your child mathematics and the importance of saving. With the coins in a piggy bank, you can teach your child counting, subtraction or addition. If you are using a piggy bank to teach younger children math, make sure to count the coin loudly as they drop in the till. Older children can learn addition by adding up the money they have collected. They can also learn subtraction by removing a certain amount from the money to buy something.

70. BBC Bitesize

There are many potential outlets for supporting the framework your child is being taught at school in their Mathematics lessons (and English too). One option available to you is BBC Bitesize. This platform is excellent for fun, educational, informative and challenging activities for your children, no matter what exam they are preparing for. Mostly focusing on Mathematics, English and key subjects, this can be a fresh approach to learning that incorporates digital technology in a more positive way.

4

TEACHING YOUR KIDS ENGLISH AT HOME

Why Should Children be Taught English at an Early Stage?

If I asked you how you learnt and became fluent in your mother tongue, what would your answer be? I'm sure you'd tell me that you are fluent in your language because you started learning it since you were a child. You should also teach your child English in a similar manner so that your child can gain enough practice and be fluent.

What are the Benefits of teaching your child English from an early age?

- It makes the child more exposed.
- It helps children develop a habit of communicating in English.
- Learning a foreign language offers cognitive benefits such as enhanced memory, problem-solving skills, increased creativity, the flexibility of mind and network critical thinking.
- Cultural enrichment
- Better access to information on the internet

- Higher academic achievement.

A lot of parents want to teach English to their kids at home but they are unsure of how and where to start. Teaching English to your child at home doesn't require you to be perfect or have a degree in the English language. The essential thing is that you are zealous and you encourage your children. Do not fret or worry when and if your child doesn't speak the language immediately, your child will need some time to learn the language. Teach them and be patient with them and you will find that they will speak the language in their own time.

Children learn a new language easily and quickly at a prime age. If you want your child to be well versed in spoken English, then start teaching him at an early age. Take advantage of the early teaching years and immerse your child in English language. Ensure that you incorporate spoken English into your child's daily routine to facilitate an extensive vocabulary.

Here are some ways to teach your child English language at home.

71. Establish a routine

Create time for English lessons at home. It's better to have short but frequent sessions than having long and not frequent sessions. Fifteen minutes is enough to teach your young child the English language on a daily basis. As your child gets older, you can gradually make the session longer. Make sure to keep the activities varied and short in a bid to grab the attention of your child. Make sure to carry out certain activities at the same time on a daily basis. Children feel more confident and comfortable when they can predict what to expect. For example, you can develop a routine of reading an English story to your child before bedtime or playing an English game after school every day. If your home is spacious, you can create an English space to keep things that are related to English such as games, books or DVDs. Keep in mind that repetition is necessary as children want to hear phrases or words before they can produce them on their own.

72. Playing games

Studies have shown that children learn when the activity is fun and exciting. Flashcard is a great way to teach children vocabulary and there are several games you can play alongside flashcards. They include; Happy Families, Kim's game, Snap or Memory. Also, there are several other games to play with your child to help her learn English.

- Board games - Snakes and ladders and other traditional games
- Action games - What's the time Mr. Wolf? Charades and Simon says.
- Word games - Hangman, I spy.

73. Using everyday situations

The advantage of teaching your child English at home is that you can use real objects and everyday situations to learn and practice the language in context and naturally.

For example:

- Talk to your child about clothes when you are arranging laundry or when your child is getting dressed.
- Teach your child vocabulary for furniture and toys when you are tidying up the room.
- Teach your child food vocabulary when you are shopping at the grocery store or when you are cooking. When next you go to the supermarket or a store, give your child the list of groceries to find. When you get home, revise the

vocabulary as you are putting the groceries in the appropriate places.

74. Using stories

Young children are attracted to books with attractive illustrations and bright colours. Identify the pictures together and pronounce the words as you identify the pictures. After reading, you can ask your child to point to different pictures. For example, ask your child to point to the picture of a cat. Also, encourage learning by asking him to pronounce the words. Reading stories to your child will get him familiar with the rhythms and sounds of English.

75. Using songs

A song is an effective way to teach children pronunciations and new words. Songs that are actionable are suitable for young children since they can demonstrate even if they are unable to sing the song. Your child can use hand gestures to demonstrate the meaning of the words mentioned in the song. Schools should resist putting additional time and resources into yet more English and maths lessons and instead give children's learning a research-evidenced boost by encouraging them to join a band or an orchestra, says **Martin Leigh**.

76. Teaching grammar

When teaching young children English language at home, you need not teach grammar rules explicitly. Instead, make sure that they are used to hearing and using grammatical structures in different contexts. For example, 'must or mustn't', when you are talking about home or school rules and 'have got' when you are talking about the appearance of a person. Learning how grammatical structures are used in different contexts from an early age goes a long way in helping your child to apply it correctly and naturally when they grow older. When your young child grows older, she can in turn teach her siblings or friends how to use grammatical structures in different contexts. While your older child is teaching others how to use grammar, she is also teaching herself further.

77. Which phrases and words should I teach first?

Consider the personality and interest of your child when deciding the topics to teach your child. Also, you can ask your child to help you select the topics to teach. You may start teaching with some of these topics:

- Numbers (1–10; 10–20; 20–100).
- Adjectives (e.g. big, small, tall, happy, sad, tired).
- Colours
- Part of the body
- toys
- clothes
- animals (e.g. pets, farm animals, wild animals)
- food

It's vital that you use the same phrase with your child every time so your child can get familiar with English Time language. Use phrases such as "It's English time" "Shall we sit down", "which book or story should we start with today?" Over time, your child will pick up phrases such as thank you, please, identify, where is? point to, it's, I don't like, I like, what's the name of?, what colour is it?

Regardless of the approach you use, the most important thing is to make English time a relaxing fun and enjoyable time for you and your child.

78. Have 'English only' days in your home

All children enjoy playing games, most especially games that bring about a friendly competition between siblings. Set aside a day in the week to be an 'English only' day in your home. This means that English is the only allowed language on English only days. Set aside a small jar and place in a conspicuous area such as kitchen counter for anyone who speaks a language that is different to English language to drop a marble. At the end of the day, count the number of marbles in the jar and declare the child with the least amount of marvels the winner of the competition.

79. Play 'rainy day' games

Rainy day games are referred to as the easy and quick games you can play without using many materials. A perfect example of such a game is Hangman. Hangman is a quick and easy game that will get your child to spell and communicate in English. The materials needed to play hangman are simply a pencil and paper. Another activity that encourages English speaking is creating a story. Creating a story is ideal for a small group. You will have each child write her name at the top right corner of a piece of paper with the title "once upon a time". Have each child pass their paper to the next person on the left. Each child will write the first sentence of the story, fold the paper and pass to the next person. Make sure that the children do not see the written first sentences. Have them write the second sentence of the story, fold the paper and then pass to the next person. The cycle continues until the papers get to the original owners. After each child must have completed the story, have them read the story aloud. Children enjoy playing this game, as such, they will want to play again and again. It's a fun and creative way to teach your children spoken English without living the comfort of your living room.

80. Watch a movie in English

Let technology and media work to your advantage. Give your child the opportunity to choose a movie to watch in English. Pause the movie occasionally to ask questions such as, "Why do you think a particular character said a statement" "How do you think the movie is going to end?" At the end of the movie, ask your child his favourite part and his least favourite part and have him answer in English. Further to teaching children to speak English, watching movies in English also introduces children to a wide variety of vocabulary contexts, phrases and words. Also, English movies help to internalise the right English pronunciation in children. Set aside a night to watch an English movie in a week. Watch English movie with your child the same night every week. To make it more fun and exciting, have the child who wins the English only day to choose the English movie to watch on English movie nights. These fun activities will encourage your children to speak English fluently.

81. Hire an English speaking nanny/babysitter

Hire an English speaking nanny/babysitter to teach your child on nights when you need to work shifts or leave your children at home. Both your child and you will benefit from hiring an English speaking nanny/babysitter. How? You will be at ease wherever you know that your child is having an exciting and educational evening. A child's nanny/babysitter is someone who takes care of children when the parents or other members of the family are not available. They care for the basic needs of children such as feeding and bathing. They also organise activities that will allow children to learn more about the world and identify their interests. Unlike parents or siblings, English language may be the only language that a nanny/babysitter under-stands. This will drive your children to put more efforts into speaking English in a bid to communicate fluently with the caregiver. While your child is gradually making efforts to communicate with the nanny/babysitter, she is also improving her English speaking abilities.

82. Play online educational computer games

There are quite a number of free educational games to help teach children English Language. These educational games are useful tools or resources to teach children spoken English. Many of such games speak to your child in English, thus teaching him words pronunciation. These games speak to your child and show him pictures at the same time. This method of teaching provides context and also repeat words thereby helping your child pronounce the repeated words correctly. These educational games are perfect for children who are just learning vocabulary, new to vocabulary or not familiar with in-depth vocabulary. After entertaining with a game a few times, your children will have a better understanding of what a myriad of vocabulary words relate to, although he might not know the meaning of the words.

When you teach your child spoken English using the discussed methods, you can be rest assured that your child will learn to speak English without thinking. Don't just practice these methods and stop. After trying these activities or methods, ask your child for the activities they enjoyed and the ones they didn't enjoy. Do not be discouraged and don't stop teaching. A little English practise every day will combine to give your child a head start needed to master the English language later on.

5

HOMEWORK & STUDY SKILLS

How to assist your child in developing good study habits

Good study habits are not inbuilt in a child, they are learnt. As a parent, creating a daily and weekly plan for your child can help him have an understanding of what she needs to study. Likewise, giving your child rewards for every task she accomplishes can help her study hard and effectively since she is aware that there's a beautiful reward at the end of it. Good study habits do not come to a child naturally or easily, children needs to be taught good study habits to develop them. This can be hard for a parent who is unsure of how to get involved in a child's homework.

It's expedient for parents to learn effective study strategies as it helps to reduce the stress children face at school and also improve their grades. Efficient study strategies can also come in handy while your child is doing homework to avoid struggles. Your child needs to know that there is more to studying than just sitting down to revise notes. You need to teach your child that studying entails knowing what to study, the time to study and keeping track of tests and assignments.

A number of teachers list daily assignments as well as due dates. Your kid can use this to plan his study time. Here are some tips you can teach your child to develop good study habits.

83. Create a calendar

Teach your child how to use the calendar to track assignments; teach your child how to mark dates on calendars with a marker to keep track of assignments. She can mark dates with due dates for appointments, activities and assignments on a calendar with different coloured markers. Also, you can teach your child how to use online calendar sync with his laptop or smartphone.

84. Create a weekly planner

Teach your kids how to use a calendar to prepare a study plan for the week. With a calendar, show your child how to transfer her obligations from a calendar to a weekly planner, ensuring that he includes time to work on the assignments before the due dates. You can also teach her to download a weekly list from her online calendar.

85. Create a daily checklist.

Though creating a checklist may seem like a daunting task, creating a checklist from the weekly plan is very helpful. The daily checklist or daily to-do-list will help your child to keep track of his daily activities and also see the progress she's making. Encourage your child to list her daily tasks in the order of importance and she should do the task accordingly.

86. "CHECK" into studying.

Once your child has figured out what to study, the next step is to learn how to study. Learning how to study can be broken down into a "CHECK" list with each letter standing for a step in the process of learning how to study.

87. Consider location.

What location works best for your child? Is it the library, at home or the tuition centre? While some teens work better without distractions, other teens like to have someone with them just in case they need help. Make an effort so that your child studies or does his homework in the location he chooses.

88. Have all materials handy

Looking for a calculator or a pencil when studying can cause a distraction. As such, it's your duty to help your child set aside a place to keep his homework materials so they are always available to use once she starts studying.

89. Establish rewards.

Establish rewards to motivate your child when she's studying. For instance, for every chapter she reads, you might allow her to use the computer for 15 minutes. When you make giving rewards a habit, she will eventually learn how to reward herself. She could snack between algebra and English homework.

90. Create a study checklist.

A study checklist includes all the steps your child needs to follow to study daily and to do her homework. A study checklist lists all the steps and this makes it easier for her to get started on her task and also manage her time. Likewise, a study checklist will make her homework seem less daunting than it is.

91. Keep a worry pad.

A worry pad is a tool designed for children who are easily carried away by their own thoughts. Rather than get carried away with the distracting things that pop into her head, instead she should write them on the worry pad to deal with them later after she's done studying.

92. Know the teachers

Relate to your child's teachers. Attend school events like parent evenings to sit and socialise with your child's teachers. Ask questions about their homework and how you can get involved.

93. Make your home a homework-friendly environment

Ensure that your home is friendly enough for your child to write and complete her homework. Also, keep supplies such as pencils, scissors, papers and glue within reach.

94. Reduce distractions

Reduce distractions such as loud music, phone calls or TV. Though a phone call to a classmate asking about an assignment is helpful.

95. Ensure that your kids do their homework on their own

Your child will not learn if he doesn't think for himself and make mistakes. Make yourself available to direct your child and make suggestions. You need to understand that it's the duty of your child to do the learning.

96. Be a monitor and a motivator

Ask your child about tests, quizzes and assignments. Make sure to check completed homework, encourage your child and be available to answer questions.

97. Lead by example

Has your child ever seen you reading a book or balancing your budget? Studies have shown that children follow the examples of their parents more than the advice they give.

98. Praise their work and efforts.

Praise the work and efforts of your child. Post an aced project or test on the refrigerator for every member of the family to see. Mention your child's academic achievement to friends and relatives.

99. Encourage your child to think positively

Encourage your kid to have a positive mindset towards studying as a positive mindset make a difference. Help your child change negative statements such as "I will never get a good grade in this subject" to "I started studying later than expected and I'm convinced that I'll get a good grade in the exam."

100. Teach your child active reading

It's easy for your child to skim through a book chapter without having an idea of what the chapter is all about. Teach your child active reading by encouraging her to note down the main idea of a chapter and also search for the meaning of unfamiliar concepts or words.

Steve is a young boy who reads through text books in minutes, once he told his mum that he has got the gist of the book as he drops it but mum notices that he has not applied the knowledge so mum was being thorough with him as she helped him with it by reading through each line, this is essential here. He was able to jot down the points and when he finished this, he was asked to close his book and try to remember all that he can remember from what he had read. He was not able to remember much, so mum made him repeat the process again and again deliberately and he was now able to remember, practically all that he had read. This lesson not only helped him for the immediate but also became an habits as he did that more, he began to change in his understanding and comprehending what is being read. He does his reading after supper each day and before the mum knew it she had had trained the child to have appetite for reading which has stayed with him. He also stopped reading and snacking as an habit he had formed which made him to lack concentration while reading.

101. Review the strategies for taking a test

It's natural for your child to feel stressed days or hours before taking a test or an exam. However, there are some strategies you can teach your child to help her deal with stress and be at her best during the exam. First, ensure that your child gets settled on time for the exam and is well relaxed. Encourage her to read all the instructions on the test or exam paper so she doesn't feel rushed.

There was a story of a boy called Stanley, who was well prepared for his 11plus exam, an exam taken by 11 years old in year 6 in the United Kingdom to get into the grammar school. Stanley had worked hard and practised all the past questions available as at the time, so when he got into the exam hall, he quickly saw that the comprehension and verbal reasoning that he was to answer was one of the exact past papers he had practised with mum at home, as he started answering the questions he was so relaxed knowing that he would do well but he was not sure of an instruction on the paper and he asked the invigilator who wrongly advised him not to do that part of the paper and he had initially consented to the invigilator but just a few minutes before the exam was to be over he remembered that his tuition centre teacher had told him to go through written instruction carefully and do what he has understood from it, this made him now to start having a go at the questions.

Doing home work with them also helps prepare them for test and exams so that they do not cheat in exams or test.

A child once told the parents not to come for her parents evening to get the feedback of her yearly report because she did badly. Her parents were so much concerned that she gets good result in all her subjects in class and she was just not getting it that way in exam, this made her both parents always on her case, so to relieve herself from them she told her best friend in class so that one helps her by allowing her to cheat or copy her work during class test but when it came to final exam she could not have a go to do well and meet the parents expectations, so she decided that they don't come for her final parent's evening but they did and discovered all that has been going on, the parents initially went to school to defend their child's behaviour, but they saw for themselves, what some children are in school is completely different to what they are at home and most teachers will give an honest view of what they have seen there in school and not what is not seen.

So they helped her to start preparing for the exams even after all the preparation she still failed, but this was still good because it reveals what a great gap that was missing and they try to accept her and work with her till she was still able to get the expected grades.

The parents got good counsel which was now able to constrain their child in a particular path of which helped to train her deliberately. It is not good to put pressure on children for grades. Some children cheat because they are scared of getting bad result, so since parent value education more than anything, they cheat and make parents happy.

Do you wonder how a low ability boy who played PlayStation all through the weekend got 100% in an end of term Maths assessment, they played smart. This is the time to train children to be deligent at their work but he that must teach diligence must also be diligent.

The early years of a child's life is usually formed by mums so a child that is left alone will bring the mother shame. Steve mum remembers this all the time from the grand mother. The mum changed her job to be more available for her, she will ask her daily about what she has done at school and be interested in it.

If her child is reading a book at school, she will read the book ahead to get ready to answer the questions of the child. She was not an expert in the subject but just enough to be able to help her child.

When she comes across a topic she did not understand then she will call a tutor to teach the child that topic and print out question on the topic to verify that the topic is well understood by the child, or better still she will ask her friend or tutor to teach her and once she gets it she then transfers the knowledge to her child, most young children prefer to be taught by mums.

She did not have to know all the subject but she was just interested with her child's learning, just that simple interest will help your child willing to learn. If you get a tutor watch what is being done, so sad to say that Mrs Jones employed teachers for her son but she was never there to ensure that teaching was taking place, guess what was happening before, child was only gisting with the tutor for a paid one hour lesson, it is not enough to get a teacher you must follow through what is being taught as well.

Misbehaving in school can seriously be traced to a lot of the missing links from home even though a lot of people will like to blame school system for everything, parents have a major part to play. They had thought that they will have ready all by just taking the child to school but it does not work that way, we all have to learn to give clear instruction, correction and modelling.

102. Enrol your child in a tuition Center to fill learning gaps

Enrolling your child in tuition also helps to improve his learning. At T.C.E.C, we have helped thousands of students understand what they were taught in class but didn't understand. Some students do not understand what they are taught in class; this could be as a result of disruption or distraction, absence in class, sickness, failure to understand the concept, missed classes or not having a permanent teacher. These are a few reasons why students fall back in learning and need to fill lesson gaps. Learning gaps develop in students for many reasons, hence the urgent need to fill the gap and good learning centres do an excellent job in this. Most teens, most notably the girls choose when to listen to teachers, and many of them do not listen because they do not like the teacher. This is one of the many reasons why parents enrol children at tuition centres so they can learn missed principles. It's crucial that you ask your child if she's happy with the teacher, otherwise she won't pay attention or listen to the teacher and go about daydreaming. Once your child is happy with the teacher, she will pay attention and concentrate and then be able to understand the topics.

While some children like to do homework and get more sheets of homework to consolidate learning through repetition, others do not insist on homework and do not like repetition. As such, it's essential for parents to understand that children are different and what works for A will not work for B. It's up to professional teachers to do what is right by accurately assessing the need of a child and working out a plan that will help the child achieve predicted grades.

103. My Maths, BBC Bitesize and More

As mentioned previously, platforms like BBC Bitesize can be very beneficial to supporting your child's learning when they are at home. Particularly when they are studying for an exam, this can reinforce critical areas of knowledge where they feel they may be hazy. My Maths is purely focused on Mathematics but presents games in an entertaining way, using some very well known IPs too, for instance Deal or No Deal and Countdown.

One mother told me how her sons and daughters religiously used My Maths, physics and chemistry tutor .com (for past exam questions with work through answers) and BBC Bitesize when they were in secondary school and the resources that were on the sites had a significantly positive effect on their exam preparation. Allowing them to fill in the missing gaps in their knowledge and put them at ease before they went into the exam hall for what would have otherwise been a very stressful experience.

104. Combating Negative Behaviour

Especially when your child is at home, this is when they'll express the most negativity about school and learning. It's essential to squash those thoughts and feelings as early as you can and ensure they stay on track in their educational journeys.

It's so easy for your child to speak negatively about school, homework and learning and then choose to spend the rest of their night on technology - whether it's social media on their mobile phones or getting a couple of hours of gaming on the Xbox One. It's important where possible to discourage this though and attempt to encourage them to continue learning and expanding their knowledge base.

There are various ways you can attempt to do this; one of which is by attempting to show them that you are as passionate about their learning experience as they should be, and therefore it's not just learning, it's bonding time too.

If your child sees learning as a time to bond with their parents too, they may see it in a more positive way, especially if you can find a way of presenting the information in a more exciting and fun way than their teachers could have. Another reason they may be more inclined to learn this way at home maybe if you see it as way more informal than the traditional classroom setting - appear chilled out about it and they will similarly act in the same manner. Make learning at home into something it usually isn't - make it fun, relaxed, natural and where possible, entertaining.

It's going to be so easy for your child to reach for the Xbox One controller when they get home from school, but show them that distractions will not benefit them in later life. Though, this can't always be the case, and therefore ensure that their weekends are free from work and either for family time or at least downtime where they are able to go on games consoles if they wish to.

One father once told me of his child who hated school so much that when he got home after a long day of learning, he would shut himself in his bedroom and refuse to come off his games console. His father felt terrible because his son clearly wanted an escape from his difficult days at school, but he knew that the reason his son was finding it so difficult at school was because he wasn't reinforcing his learning from school in his free time after school, therefore he was falling behind and feeling inadequate in comparison to his peers. It was a self-caused vicious cycle. The only time he saw a positive change was when he finally confiscated the games console until his son's grades started to improve.

Though this method may not work for everybody, it should be noted that if you're feeling backed into a corner and like there's no other choice, it's probably because there isn't another choice. If you need to confiscate negatively-impacting technology from your children in order for them to see improvements in their work, then by all means go for it.

It's worth noting however that in a recent survey, almost half of students said that technology for non-educational purposes was distracting [14] so bear that in mind.

105. Managing Your Child's Time Online

Navigating cyberspace can be stressful enough for adults to even comprehend, now imagine what that is like for a child who is vulnerable to all kinds of danger when using the internet. It's essential that you not only support their journey through the treacherous waters of the internet but also navigate alongside them in order to protect and support them as best you can.

Encourage healthy use of digital technology, encourage them to not use technology as a distraction but to use it for its real benefits - education.

The last thing you want is your child to face the real dangers online, or for them to become addicted to digital distractions, so set them on the right path while learning at home, ensure their homework is as reliable and persuasive as it can possibly be and ensure they feel supported in their educational journeys.

If you feel it necessary, set parental controls and filters on the family computers and digital devices. Observe their conversations on the internet and monitor them in any way you deem appropriate. There's no such thing as being too safe when it comes to looking after your children as they navigate cyberspace.

When it comes to the uncertain world of the internet, there should be no such thing as hands-off parenting, as it will only lead to disaster.

The unique and positive culture of the T.C.E.C centre

At the T.C.E.C centre, we have a qualified teacher take a maximum of 5 students with modern technological facilities to improve learning thereby making it exciting for students to come in after school even on Saturdays.

Ever since the tuition centre began operations, thousands of students in the borough have experienced tremendous educational improvement in their grades as principles have been enacted to help children learn and focus, hence the reason for this book.

The TCEC centre in Hackney has produced excellent GCSE, IGCSE and SATs result every year without fail. At the centre, we teach children between the ages of 6-16 years old reading, English language, English literature, mathematics and spelling. Of course, there are other learning centres that run the same course but it's essential for parents to check the one that suits the child and will bring out the best in him/her. The learning centres use different methods to achieve tremendous results so the method that worked for a child might not work for the other child.

Jack is a smart boy but the learning method he isn't used to is the learning method he is exposed to. As such, he finds it difficult to understand his teachers and he fidget every time. He came to the centre and we introduce him to a step by step program of learning to help him focus on learning activities with rapt attention. His parents were delighted with his progress because he had appeared to be someone who isn't interested in learning activities. He significantly improved at the centre and he moved up 3 grades in just two months. His sister on the other hand prefer the traditional method of learning which made her slow but when she started at the learning centre, she improved and was always eager to do her homework. She is now able to organize herself to carry out her tasks and no longer reluctant to do her homework. Since she used one month to learn addition and two months to learn subtraction, one would think that she would use an additional three months to master timetable but no, Sophia learnt timetable in three weeks. This made division easy for her and when she sat for her SAT test, she had an outstanding result. We worked with her for 80 minutes every week; she had all As' in her GSCE.

A lot of parents expect to see changes in their children within 2-3 weeks of enrolling them in a learning centre. A child who has suffered a considerable learning gap will struggle with learning initially. Parents should understand that children are different and must be treated differently. In the past years, we have developed different lesson plans for children and we have also provided their lesson needs and taught children the best way of learning in order to enhance their learning process.

PLEASE LEAVE A 1-CLICK REVIEW!

Thank you for reading this book and engaging in the next step to establish healthy and effective child learning. I hope these tips help you in the same way they have helped many others.

I would really appreciate if you could take 60 seconds to write a short review for this book, even if it's just a few sentences!

Your help in spreading the word is greatly appreciated. Reviews from readers like you make a huge difference in helping new readers find helpful books like this one. I joyfully read every single review.

Just click on the link below and you will be taken straight to the review page.

Thank you!

Bukky Ekine Ogunlana

101 Tips

for

Helping With
Your Child's
Learning

Proven Strategies for Accelerated Learning and Raising
Smart Children Using Positive Parenting Skills

BUKKY EKINE-OGUNLANA

Review Book Here

CONCLUSION

Thank you for buying the book - 101 Tips for Helping with Your child's learning. I hope this book has taught you different strategies, methods and ways to help your child's learning. Parenting is a noble calling and raising children who are successful both at home and school is not an easy task. I hope this book will make your duty as a parent to make your child successful at school less daunting. I hope that this book will make your dream of raising a brilliant and well-behaved student come true.

Remember, the best students at school are not the ones who simply study before an exam or can just write a good essay, the best students are the ones who are willing to put the work in daily in order to succeed. Your children cannot achieve this alone though, and that is the message you should take away from this book. Your role in their learning is just as important as their role.

Help guide their educational journeys and reinforce the lessons they are being taught at school and you're well on your way to effectively assisting with your child's journey to learning and success.

Whether you're training your child for a life as a scientist, writer, doctor or even actor, understand what skills they need and help keep them on track.

Before you go off and help your children with their educational journeys, please do leave us some feedback for the book. Whether it's a review out of five or genuine, constructive feedback on what you liked, disliked or would have taken a different approach with. Let us know!

Now, here's to your children turning out to be future leaders and pioneers in their respective fields!

Cheers!!!

OTHER BOOKS YOU'LL LOVE!

1. Spelling One: An Interactive Vocabulary & Spelling Workbook for 5-Year-Olds (With Audiobook Lessons)

2. Spelling Two: An Interactive Vocabulary & Spelling Workbook for 6-Year-Olds (With Audiobook Lessons)

3. Spelling Three: An Interactive Vocabulary & Spelling Workbook for 7-Year-Olds (With Audiobook Lessons)

4. Spelling Four: An Interactive Vocabulary & Spelling Workbook for 8-Year-Olds (With Audiobook Lessons)

5. Spelling Five: An Interactive Vocabulary & Spelling Workbook for 9-Year-Olds (With Audiobook Lessons)

6. Spelling Six: An Interactive Vocabulary & Spelling Workbook for 10 & 11 Year-Olds (With Audiobook Lessons)

7. Spelling Seven: An Interactive Vocabulary & Spelling Workbook for 12-14 Year-Olds (With Audiobook Lessons)

8. Raising Boys in Today's Digital World: Proven Positive Parenting Tips for Raising Respectful, Successful and Confident Boys

9. Raising Girls in Today's Digital World: Proven Positive Parenting Tips for Raising Respectful, Successful and Confident Girls

10. Raising Kids in Today's Digital World: Proven Positive Parenting Tip for Raising Respectful, Successful and Confident Kids

11. The Child Development and Positive Parenting Master Class 2-in-1 Bundle: Proven Methods for Raising Well-Behaved and Intelligent Children, with Accelerated Learning Methods

12. Parenting Teens in Today's Challenging World 2-in-1 Bundle: Proven Methods for Improving Teenager's Behaviour with Positive Parenting and Family Communication

13. Life Strategies for Teenagers: Positive Parenting, Tips and Understanding Teens for Better Communication and a Happy Family

14. Parenting Teen Girls in Today's Challenging World: Proven Methods for Improving Teenager's Behaviour with Whole Brain Training

YOUR FREE GIFT!

As a way of saying thank your for
purchasing this book, I am
offer offering you a free
parenting book!

You can click on the link
below or you can wait until
the end of the book to collect
and download your free
copy.

**DOWNLOAD
YOUR FREE COPY
HERE**

REFERENCES

1. http://www.pownallgreen.stockport.sch.uk/wp-content/uploads/2014/07/Helping-your-child-learn.pdf
2. https://www.linkedin.com/pulse/benefits-helping-children-homework-elliott-shostak
3. https://www2.ed.gov/parents/academic/help/homework/
4. https://www.babycentre.co.uk/a6509/developmental-milestones-hearing
5. https://freekidsbooks.org/wp-content/uploads/2016/12/Teaching-Children-to-Read.pdf
6. http://www.parentingcounts.org/information/documents/talking-to-baby-100-705-200907.pdf
7. http://ftp.iza.org/dp7416.pdf
8. https://ryanlanz.com/2015/05/06/why-you-should-encourage-your-children-to-tell-stories/
9. https://ahrc.eq.edu.au/ourservices/Documents/rc-parent-booklet.pdf

10. https://centerforparentingeducation.org/library-of-articles/focus-parents/role-model-promise-peril/

11. https://mrswintersbliss.com/fiction-vs-nonfiction-teaching-ideas/

12. https://pdfs.semanticscholar.org/aed9/5c4d2b4ddb11d4199e4ab91ac0ee41fb2219.pdf

13. https://www.cameverlands.org.uk/10-benefits-of-reading/

14. https://www.insidehighered.com/digital-learning/article/2019/07/10/survey-shows-nearly-half-students-distracted-technology

USEFUL WEBSITES:

1. http://taylorda01.weebly.com/increasingly-difficult-questions.html - really good for increasingly difficult questions

2. www.mathsbot.com – brilliant GCSE styles questions http://www.mrbartonmaths.com/teachers/ - endless amounts of resources

3. https://justmaths.co.uk/2015/12/21/9-1-exam-questions-by-topic-higher-tier/ - exam style questions for higher tier (worked solutions as well)

4. https://justmaths.co.uk/2015/11/29/9-1-exam-questions-by-topic-foundation-version-2/ - exactly the same as above but for foundation

5. https://www.missbsresources.com/ - some useful revision mats

6. https://www.resourceaholic.com/ - lots of resources and thought provoking activities

7. http://bland.in/edexcel_9-1.html - exam questions

8. https://www.mathsgenie.co.uk/ - past papers

9. https://corbettmaths.com/contents/ - exam style questions

10. https://www.maths4everyone.com/ - lots of loop cards, exam questions

11. https://www.accessmaths.co.uk/ - some great starters on here and lots of other resources

12. https://www.teachitmaths.co.uk/ - lots of different activities

13. https://www.cimt.org.uk/projects/mep/index.htm - challenging worded problems

14. https://www.math-salamanders.com/ - some useful worksheets (have to have a hunt)

15. https://nrich.maths.org/ - brilliant problem solving resources and thought provoking activities